Praise for the plays of Doug Wright

INTERROGATING THE NUDE

"[A] campy cerebral thriller."   —Patrick Pacheco, *Los Angeles Times*

"Imaginative and intellectually daring."
                                —Robert Viagas, *The Advocate* (Stamford)

"A tongue-in-cheek speculation on the circumstances surrounding the creation of Duchamp's controversial cubist painting *Nude Descending a Staircase*, the play combines a knowledge of art history with theater savvy."   —Tom Killen, *New Haven Register*

"A delicious mix of comedy, sex and mystery."
                                —Janice Page, *The Providence Journal*

"Fascinating."   —Edgar Kloten, *West Hartford News*

"Keeps audiences guessing—and laughing—right up to the final . . . curtain."   —Tom Caruso, *Journal Inquirer* (Manchester, Conn.)

WATBANALAND

"Wright has written what looks on the surface like yet another satire-critique of bourgeois angst about a yup couple who can't have a child. But things lurk below that surface . . . Wright has actually managed to find something people don't want to think about or talk about, or even admit, really: their fears of their own coming children, their rage at these future replacements and terror at what their offspring might reveal about their parents' true, hidden selves."
                                                    —Lloyd Rose, *The Washington Post*

"Wright's writing uses sitcom as a matrix, the way Stoppard uses comedy of manners . . . *Watbanaland* sticks to your ribs, creepily, as if barbecue sauce were being painted on them."
                                            —Michael Feingold, *The Village Voice*

"Blisteringly immediate."   —Bob Mondello, *Washington City Paper*

"[*Watbanaland*] takes a number of wacky, disturbing turns as it builds on themes of giving life . . . An artful grotesquerie."
                                            —Nelson Pressley, *The Washington Times*

QUILLS

"Astonishingly smart . . . *Quills* is that rare play that is grotesque only out of necessity for its themes, a play that is at once very funny and profoundly disturbing. Imagine a Grand Guignol dressed up as a Restoration comedy, held together by beautiful writing and a passionate idea. Clearly the playwright stands for free speech, but he has no easy arguments. Wright insists that the cost of free speech can be frightening, but the playwright shows that the cost of censorship is even more horrifying, and in unexpected ways."
                                            —Laurie Winer, *Los Angeles Times*

"Cunningly structured and gorgeously written, with every phrase turned to a high, gleaming polish . . . *Quills* is a superb piece of writing." —Michael Feingold, *The Village Voice*

"Part theater of the ridiculous, part comedy of manners and part Grand Guignol . . . [*Quills*] successfully blends intentional archness, grotesque exaggeration and bold humor to create a theatrical experience of real wit." —Vincent Canby, *The New York Times*

"Sensational in every sense of the word . . . [A] testament both to the power of words and to the indomitability of genius—even depraved genius . . . Amazing." —Jeremy Gerard, *Variety*

"A cuttingly intelligent rumination on free speech." —Louise Kennedy, *The Boston Globe*

"Virulently witty, [*Quills*] wades fearlessly into dangerous thematic waters . . . vividly dramatiz[ing] the war between artistic freedom and societal repression." —Alexis Greene, *TheaterWeek*

"In its take-no-prisoners way, [*Quills*] raises some essential questions about the hypocrisy of moral authority and, most crucially, the relationship between artist and audience." —Clifford A. Ridley, *The Philadelphia Inquirer*

"[A] potent black comedy." —Everett Evans, *Houston Chronicle*

"Wrathfully, gluttonously—almost sinfully—theatrical, *Quills* . . . is exhilarating." —Lloyd Rose, *The Washington Post*

DOUG WRIGHT

Quills and Other Plays

Doug Wright received the Pulitzer Prize for Drama and the Tony Award for Best Play for *I Am My Own Wife*. He won an Obie Award for outstanding achievement in playwriting and the Kesselring Award for Best New American Play from the National Arts Club for his play *Quills*, which he then adapted into a screenplay, making his motion-picture debut. The film was named best picture by the National Board of Review and nominated for three Academy Awards. His screenplay was nominated for a Golden Globe Award and received the Paul Selvin Award from the Writers Guild of America. Wright's stage work has been produced at the New York Theatre Workshop, Lincoln Center, the WPA Theater, The Vineyard, Geffen Playhouse, Wilma, Woolly Mammoth, the McCarter Theater, and La Jolla Playhouse. His previous works include *The Stonewater Rapture*, *Buzzsaw Berkeley*, and *Unwrap Your Candy*. Wright has been published three times in the *Best Short Plays* series, and his work has appeared in the *Paris Review*. In 2004, he received a special career citation from the American Academy of Arts and Letters. He's a member of the Dramatists Guild; the Writers Guild of America, East; and the Society of Stage Directors and Choreographers. He serves on the board of the New York Theatre Workshop.

ALSO BY DOUG WRIGHT

I Am My Own Wife

AND OTHER PLAYS

Quills

AND OTHER PLAYS

Doug Wright

FABER AND FABER, INC.

An affiliate of Farrar, Straus and Giroux

New York

Faber and Faber, Inc.
An affiliate of Farrar, Straus and Giroux
19 Union Square West, New York 10003

Interrogating the Nude was first published in 1992 in *New American Plays One* by Heinemann Drama; *Watbanaland* was first published in 1995 by Dramatists Play Service, Inc.; *Quills* was first published in 1996 by Dramatists Play Service, Inc.

Library of Congress Cataloging-in-Publication Data
Wright, Doug, 1962–
    Quills and other plays / Doug Wright. — 1st ed.
        p. cm.
    ISBN-13: 978-0-571-21180-7 (pbk. : alk. paper)
    ISBN-10: 0-571-21180-1 (pbk. : alk. paper)
    1. Sade, Marquis de, 1740–1814—Drama.   2. Duchamp, Marcel, 1887–
1968—Drama.   3. Yuppies—Drama.   I. Title.

PS3573.R53252Q55 2005
812'.54—dc22

                                                            2005040094

Designed by Cassandra J. Pappas

www.fsgbooks.com

10   9   8   7   6   5   4   3   2   1

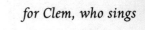

for Clem, who sings

CONTENTS

INTRODUCTION:

WILLFUL MISBEHAVIOR

FULL DISCLOSURE? I was a repressed and compulsively well-behaved Presbyterian child who grew up in Dallas, Texas. I always raised my hand before speaking, and was forever polishing proverbial apples. Beneath my modest exterior, however, lay another self altogether: a closeted gay kid, his imagination fertile with feverish, baroque fantasies and purportedly wicked thoughts.

I'll never forget one day in elementary-school art class. Now, I couldn't hit a ball or cross a finish line, but I was precocious with a paintbrush (a skill that, unfortunately, has faded with time). This particular afternoon, circa 1973, the air was filled with the odor of powdered tempera. I was seated among my peers, tow-headed boys and girls in polo shirts and state-of-the-art orthodontics. Spread before each of us were blank sheets of butcher paper. Parents' Night was scant days away, and the walls of the classroom were conspicuously bare. Our teacher needed to fill them—hastily—with student work, designed to impress our parents and to reassure them that hers was a benevolent dictatorship, one that nurtured artistic expression.

"Paint quickly," she admonished us, "and the best work will get pinned to the bulletin board."

I was breathless with excitement; it was more than just an assignment. Why, it was my first commission! Spurred by the two things I seem to require most—inspiration and a deadline—I began to paint.

My subject? At home, Mother had been reading to me nightly from her dog-eared copy of Edith Hamilton's *Mythology*, and I had become obsessed with Medusa. Like many young homosexual boys, I had already fallen fatefully in love with melodramatic excess (is anything more formative than bottled emotion?), and the Gorgon—with her mane of hissing serpents and her fatal visage—really got my heart racing.

I decided to bring her to terrible, vivid life—and not in some static, archaic pose, oh no. I would render her severed head, newly decapitated by Perseus, her expression locked in furious amazement, while a few opportunistic snakes disentangled themselves from her scalp to wriggle free. (Peter Paul Rubens had nothing on me.) My secret, unstated goal was simple: to create a portrait so fearsome that, like the monster it depicted, the viewer would turn to stone from just gazing upon it. Imagine the class bully, Arthur Stovall, or haughty Sally Fenwick glancing at my masterwork, then calcifying into rock!

(I'm convinced that children—angst-ridden adolescents in particular—will use whatever tools are placed at their disposal for self-expression. Daily, I'm thankful that my parents kept our family den stocked with watercolors and modeling clay instead of, say, hunting rifles. Better that youthful outbursts give rise to art than special reports on CNN.)

At last my painting was finished. It was still glistening when I took it up to the teacher's desk, ready for her sanction. She paused before saying a word, staring at it for a very long time. "Why, Douglas," she finally said. "It's so . . . *imaginative*."

I thrust out my prepubescent chest with pride. Surely my picture would hang prominently, in a place of honor. No matter how diligently the other students were painting, their winsome subjects—kittens and rainbows and ponies and clowns—couldn't begin to compete with mine. The sallow, gray tones of Medusa's dying flesh, the poignant crimson curve of her jugular—it was an indisputable triumph!

The teacher cleared her throat. "You'll understand—won't you?—if we save this to display at some other time?"

I knew that was certain death. My picture would never grace the bulletin board; it would be relegated to a file folder in the rear of the supply cabinet until the end of the semester, when I would be allowed to take it home.

Was I disappointed? On the contrary, I felt a surge of adrenaline. My painting was beyond artful. Why . . . it was *forbidden!* To a mild-mannered ten-year-old with dreams less in accord with Horatio Alger than Julian Beck, that carried its own unmistakable thrill. Now, years later, I still find myself chasing that illicit rush every time I sit down to write.

As a child, I flattered myself that I was a provocateur. I've mellowed with adulthood, and now I merely write about provocateurs. I'm drawn to characters who willfully, even gleefully, thwart the status quo, outsiders who subvert or expose their surroundings in a way that's entertaining, sly, and—arguably—moral (before the word became code for a new breed of religious terrorism; back when it meant "ethical" or "principled").

The characters I have chosen to depict in my work are, admittedly, an unruly, eccentric lot. But it's my conviction as a dramatist that sometimes the most extreme, seemingly marginal figures yield the most universal human truths. I have a particular enthusiasm for artists, creative men and women who place themselves in deliberate opposition to the dominant culture and challenge it. If institutions like the government and the Church exist to support and uphold societal norms, then art's chief responsibility is, I think, to rankle them.

One such subversive became the hero of my very first full-length play, *Interrogating the Nude*. I originally encountered Marcel Duchamp in an undergraduate art-history course entitled "The Machine Aesthetic." Growing up in Texas in the 1970s, my exposure to the art world was minimal, and steeped in the conventional canon. I'd seen the Remington Bronzes—cowboys on horseback, mostly— at the Amon Carter Museum in Fort Worth, and we had a few mammoth LeRoy Neiman paintings of football players on display at the neighborhood mall. But nothing had prepared me for the sheer, liberating insolence of Duchamp's oeuvre. A urinal christened *Fountain*, and slapped with the signature "R. Mutt"? A coat rack, suspended from the ceiling? Sexual allegories rendered in glass, with whirring pistons, widgets, fuse wire, and dust? Duchamp was a scamp, an enfant terrible running loose in a modernist playroom. For the first time, I realized that art could transcend the merely decorative, that it existed in an ideological as well as a visual field. It could delight the eye, of course, but it could also puncture the mind. Suffice it to say—like many a wide-eyed, wannabe art theorist—I developed a major schoolboy crush on Duchamp.

And what better mash note than a play! I began writing *Interrogating the Nude* in 1986, as my graduate thesis at New York University. It was the first time I had ever tackled the life of a famous artist. I was daunted, to be sure, so I went after it with the same studiousness that I brought to my term papers. (In those days, when I wrote a script I always began with the title space, centering it neatly and noting the date. I believed that—just like gastronomy or English landscape design—presentation was half the battle.)

As a result, my first draft was an exercise in sincerity. I recounted—with absolute fidelity to the facts—Duchamp's arrival in the New World, a pivotal moment (I presumed) in his young life. The play was structured in a series of straightforward, chronological scenes: the artist on the S.S. *Rochambeau* during his transatlantic crossing; his disembarkation at Ellis Island; his seminal first meeting with the photographer Man Ray. It was scrupulously researched, written with unimpeachable reverence for its subject, and dull beyond all measure.

In attempting to honor my protagonist, I was insulting him. Duchamp was many things—iconoclast, philosopher, dandy—but he was never tedious. And yet in my play he was little more than an encyclopedia entry. I wasn't scribing drama; I was attempting to dramatize a biography, a foolhardy endeavor. (Our lives don't have narrative and thematic continuity; that is the happy fiction that art bestows upon us, and why we need it so desperately.)

Then I had a tiny but welcome epiphany. To truly pay homage to Duchamp, I needed to emulate his art, not his life. I needed to approximate the wit and sinister whimsy that he brought to his work. I began to reread historical accounts surrounding the 1913 debut of *Nude Descending a Staircase* in New York's notorious Armory Show. The painting had caused a huge scandal; never before had the most sacred of art's subjects—the female nude—been treated with such barbaric irreverence: her body, chopped into cubist fragments, as she indecorously galumphed down a series of steps. This wasn't originality; it was desecration. There were picket lines; riots broke out among the spectators. Even President Theodore Roosevelt took a loud stance against the "immoral" picture. Its impact on the American art world was seismic; I decided to make it the focus of my plot.

Immediately I was beset by a challenge: onstage, how could I make outrage over the painting plausible? After all, Duchamp's *Nude* is markedly less shocking now than it was almost a century ago. Compared with recent works like Damien Hirst's pickled cow, Andres Serrano's *Piss Christ*, and Professor Gunther von Hagens's flayed corpses, it's downright quaint. How could I make its premiere resonate with the requisite perversity? I had to make public indignation over art a fresh idea, a first-time phenomenon, if the play was to work at all.

Turn-of-the-century critics had admonished Duchamp for "murdering art." What if I took that notion literally? What if my play weren't a biographical portrait at all but a murder mystery? It's the eve of the Armory Show; an artist's model has reportedly been dismembered, the fragments of her body left strewn across a tenement stair. But when detectives arrive to investigate, the victim's remnants have been removed, and in their place is a canvas, still wet with paint. The prime suspect: Marcel Duchamp, of course. *Perry Mason* meets Dada—a police inquiry into the very heart of European modernism.

Suddenly my mind was spinning with the same velocity as Duchamp's *Bicycle Wheel*. My play finally had a motor! And—within the familiar narrative structure of a mystery—I could pose questions central to Duchamp's oeuvre: What constitutes an aesthetic crime? What is the impact of irreverent art on public morality? Is one man's felony another man's muse? And isn't innovation always a crime against the status quo? These were more interesting questions, I reasoned, than "Where was Marcel Duchamp born?" or "Was his brother really an artist, too?"

In retrospect, it is clear to me that *Interrogating the Nude* is a youthful play; precocious (I hope!), but still the work of a writer finding his voice for the first time. Nevertheless, I have a fondness for my virgin effort. It has a brio, a nerve, and a capacity for wonder that seem to go hand in hand with naïveté. Decades of practicing my craft have made me a more painstaking writer, but sometimes I miss those glorious, heady days when the one dividend of ignorance was fearlessness (which is more tenable in art than it is in presidential politics, I hasten to add in these heedless times).

When the Yale Repertory Theater decided to produce the play in 1989, the event marked my professional playwriting debut. I'll never forget my first casting session. The halls of the theater were plastered with signs, designed to point wayward actors in the right direction. For convenience, the title of the play was abbreviated, and the signs read "NUDE Auditions This Way!" One thing I'll say for actors? They're almost always game. It made for a very memorable afternoon.

At first glance, Flo Stillman, the repressed Wasp heroine of *Watbanaland*, is the very antithesis of the outsider. What could be more mainstream, more reassuringly bourgeois, than a married woman who's eager to have a baby? Yet while Flo's aspirations may be routine, the means she employs to achieve them are not. Saddled with a chilly, distant husband and the threat of imminent menopause, Flo is forced to go to unorthodox lengths to bear a child. Her willingness to undertake the most outré methods imaginable makes her a true maverick.

After toying with the rigid story confines of a murder mystery, I was eager to try something new. I wanted to write a play that favored theme over story. In fact, I wanted the thematic underpinnings of the play to be so strong that they could justify narrative impossibilities; fantastical events, like a late-night television hostess stepping out of the screen to confront her viewer face-to-face; or an African chieftain emerging from a Frigidaire to plead for the life of his child. I hoped the resultant piece would have the feverish logic of a late-morning dream. Symbolism would be primary, and the story would follow its logic, not the other way around.

I had a secondary objective as well: to aggressively experiment with language. When critiquing one another's work, students in my playwriting classes are always quick to allege, "Real people don't talk that way!" I almost always find this remark specious. "You're right!" I tell them. "People rarely sound like Edward Albee. They rarely chat like Pinter or Mamet. If you want to hear wholly convincing, utterly naturalistic dialogue, then ride the subway. Go to a dinner party. *Don't go see a play!* But if you want to hear heightened language, enlisted for maximum literary or dramatic effect, then by all means go to the theater." In *Watbanaland*, I aimed to do just that: to create a mode of speech for each character that pushed past naturalism to a more revealing, poetic truth.

The play is about hunger in its various manifestations: sexual, physical, and spiritual. Each character has a desire so pointed, so palpable that it borders on carnivorous. Flo craves a healthy, happy child. Beneath his hostile veneer, her husband, Park, craves absolution. His secretary and onetime mistress, Marilyn, craves justice (even retribution), while her boyfriend, Dash, craves a family of his own. For Yobo Munde and his son Baku, hunger isn't a metaphor for anything; it's life threateningly real. The stories dovetail, collide, and at times even bypass one another altogether. But in their juxtaposition they illustrate common longing in the most disparate and remote circumstances.

The cannibalism referenced in the play's second act has caused some actors, directors, and audiences a certain measure of disquiet. This is hardly surprising, given the virulently racist manner in which cannibalism has usually been depicted: comic savages, their necks festooned with teeth, encircling a cauldron filled with hapless missionaries, smacking their lips in giddy anticipation of a meal. In cultures where cannibalism actually occurs—and it is an exceedingly rare phenomenon—it is the very antithesis of these crass Western imaginings. In fact, it is almost always a religious rite. In Papua New Guinea, a widow will ingest a small portion of her deceased husband's tissue in the hope that she will thereby grant him

immortality. There is evidence that certain Native Americans prac-
ticed similar rituals. And, of course, in the Last Supper Christ himself renders cannibalism a Holy Sacrament. Any Catholic who
purports to believe in transubstantiation yet professes distaste or
even horror at cannibalism is either a hypocrite or woefully ill in-
formed about the practice itself. (In his court testimony, even Jeffrey
Dahmer described his own cannibalism as an attempt at atone-
ment, not as the pursuit of some twisted culinary or sexual gratification.) The cannibalism in *Watbanaland*, I would suggest, is neither
sensationalist nor drawn from an insidious body of clichés; it is a
spiritual act. To present it as anything else is to misread the play.

Now, an author's admission: I love *Watbanaland* with a parent's
blind tenacity, but its public reception has been less wholehearted.
When it opened at the WPA Theater in New York in 1995, it was
summarily dismissed in the *New York Times*. A year later, the Woolly
Mammoth Theater Company, in Washington, D.C., gave it a brac-
ing, fearless production, and it became the critics' darling, cited by
the *Washington Post* as a truly important new work. (Like many
authors, I strenuously avoid reading the reviews of my plays. Nevertheless, the contents always trickle back to you: well-meaning
friends and relatives leave messages on your answering machine
saying "I didn't think the play was 'the worst theatrical travesty
since *Moose Murders*'" or "I don't care what the newspaper says, you
are not 'half-baked Strindberg, with an unfortunate dollop of
Danielle Steele.'" Sometimes there are even more telling signs: an
upward surge in ticket sales, or a sudden closing notice pasted on
the theater's front door.)

Pundits say that true artistes always prefer sharply oppositional
reviews to blandly uniform ones, and in theory I agree. A really vi-
tal, necessary play should incite shouting matches, not a benign "I
loved it, honey. Now, where did we park the car?" But in practice
I'm a bit less romantic than that. Unless a new work garners undis-

puted laurels, it wilts on the vine. Few theaters are courageous enough—or, more charitably, can afford—to give it a second, third, or fourth airing. As a result, the play is infrequently produced. I'm especially grateful for the inclusion of *Watbanaland* in this volume. Now from the comfort of your armchair you can embark on its dark journey, unimpeded by editorial brainwash of either an adulatory or a damning sort.

Of course, in the pantheon of miscreants, the Marquis de Sade is the grandaddy of 'em all. I knew one day we'd tango; it was only a matter of time. Writers live for those thrilling moments when the personal, aesthetic, and political all overlap. That's the fervent stew that produces art. In *Quills*, that happened for me.

On the personal front, I was drawn to Sade as a result of a love affair that went south. I had been dating a psychiatrist (not my own) for almost two years. During our final months together, he gave me Maurice Lever's engrossing and erudite biography of the divine Marquis as a Christmas gift, a gesture that titillated my intellect but worried my heart. Surely, I thought, our love affair is doomed! True enough, we separated a short time later, and I wrote *Quills* in an effort to recover from the demise of the relationship. That may sound obscure, but to me the parallels were quite clear: *Quills* is about a mental-health professional (the Abbé de Coulmier) who becomes involved with a mad, untimely writer (Sade). I was a melodramatic scribe in love with a shrink! *Quills* mirrored my own circumstances almost exactly (minus, dare I confess, the bullwhips, nipple clamps, and aniseed pastilles). In fact, many of the florid debates these two characters wage are drawn from the pillow talk I shared with my doctor friend. They've been gussied up, sure, with ten-dollar words and new historical context, but the spirit is much the same, qualifying *Quills* as a thinly disguised roman à clef.

On the aesthetic front, in Sade I found a writer who was purple, outrageous, and naughty—qualities that I strive for in my own work. I was also fascinated by the maddening inconsistency of his prose. One minute it is as puerile, moronic, and sex-obsessed as the most irresponsible pornography; the next, it is excoriating and hilarious, its targets worthy, and its barbs as well aimed as those lobbed by Jonathan Swift. Sade's writing is admirably consistent in one respect: it always reveals its author. He was, after all, a brilliant nobleman thwarted by his own base desires and forced to spend more than thirty years of his adult life incarcerated in prisons and madhouses. Sade wrote to stave off his isolation. In one chapter, he rails against his government captors, while in the next he fuels his masturbatory fantasies, a volatile blend of eroticism and stunted adolescent rage. The longer he's alone, the more extreme his fiction becomes.

Though Sade purports to write about a large range of topics—virtue and vice, the hypocrisy of the Church, the cleansing power of war—his truest subject is himself. In thousands of pages of seemingly varied text, we can divine a central, deeply haunting narrative: the increasingly shrill efforts of a man desperate to postpone the inevitable lunacy that comes with solitary confinement. Writing was Sade's attempt to preserve his own sanity, even though its content augurs madness. The Marquis's work is one of the most compelling accounts we have of a man dancing on the edge of the abyss.

On the political front, I felt that Sade's story, particularly the confiscation of his quill pens at the Charenton Asylum, offered a wonderful metaphor for what was occurring in our own culture at the time. I wrote *Quills* at the height of the art wars, when efforts to dismantle the National Endowment for the Arts were at fever pitch. The controversy began when Senator Jesse Helms stridently objected to the allocation of government funds to showcase the work of the late homoerotic photographer Robert Mapplethorpe. In the debates that ensued, Helms was cast as a latter-day Comstock, and Mapplethorpe as a brave champion of free expression.

The news media routinely depicted the two men as bitter adversaries. I never understood this characterization. To me, theirs was one of the great love stories of the twentieth century. Talk about symbiosis! The more Helms railed against the photographer, the more he ensured his own reelection in a stodgy southern state. And while Mapplethorpe wasn't alive to benefit directly from the senator's diatribes, they brought his estate unprecedented publicity. This previously little-known artist suddenly had calendars and coffee-table books for sale at Barnes & Noble! The two of them were positively stumping for each other.

The censor has always been the artist's most reliable muse; there is nothing more seductive or inspiring you can say to a would-be provocateur than "Don't do that." In Sade and Dr. Royer-Collard, I found early-nineteenth-century correlatives for the senator and the photographer. The only casualty in such an intense take-no-captives affair? In the art wars, it was the voice of moderation. And in *Quills* it's the play's lone secular humanist, the Abbé de Coulmier.

So in 1993, when I first put pen to paper to compose the play, my personal, aesthetic, and political concerns all merged to form a single story. At root, *Quills* is an incredibly simple narrative: a game of one-upmanship. The censors say "No!" so the Marquis de Sade says "Yes!" so the censors say "No!" louder, and the Marquis says "Yes!" louder, and the argument escalates in increasingly absurd ways. The play's structure is downright rudimentary, but its thematic concerns are complex. What is the impact of violent, incendiary art on the culture at large? Do we pay a higher price when we repress its expression? What happens to a toxic mind when it is denied purgation? Does government censure only invite more inventive revolt? Obviously, the play trumpets free speech, but—in its best productions—it posits some uncomfortable conservative truths as well: if art has the power to educate and even to ennoble us, can't it also corrupt? We can tolerate diverse modes of speech only if we accept both the dividends *and* the liabilities. Like it or not, art can have unexpected consequences. *Quills* takes some of the art/crime corollaries that appear in *Interrogating the Nude* and stretches them to the breaking point.

And in tone the play finds its antecedent in a certain mythological portrait, etched by an inwardly rebellious ten-year-old on a stifling day in Dallas. I'm told that my old high school keeps a copy of *Quills* in the library, but it's kept safely behind the librarian's desk. To check it out, you need a signed permission slip from your parents. Another tiny victory, thirty years later.

When I look at these three plays in sequence, I see another common denominator: rage. And I admit it without apology: I was an angry young writer. Rawboned fury is a great motivator for an artist, another reliable muse. People say that you should write about what you know, but I always say to write about what you don't know—write about what mystifies and befuddles and infuriates you. Struggle, after all, is what makes drama. Rage has always been a fertile well for me, and for countless other artists.

That said, I do find that I'm growing kinder and gentler with age. My most recent work, *I Am My Own Wife*, is probably my most compassionate to date. It is far more interested in presenting a character with all her vexing contradictions intact than in judging her actions or those of the people around her. True, Charlotte von Mahlsdorf still fits firmly in my pantheon of iconoclasts. As a transvestite who survived first the Nazis and then the Communists, she cunningly sabotaged authority and upended the norm time and again in her seventy-four years. But while I readily appropriated Sade and Duchamp as mouthpieces to express my own concerns, I resisted that temptation with Charlotte. I simply let her exist onstage. Of course, unlike my other protagonists I actually knew Charlotte, so perhaps I felt a keener obligation to let her speak for herself. This particular play was born of love as much as wrath, disenfranchisement, or stupefaction. I can't help wondering if it's mere coincidence that it is also my most successful script so far.

Perhaps I am becoming soft in my dotage. Still, I won't abandon my interest in prickly topics, societal outlaws, or the darkly perverse. Try as I might, I can't ignore the siren's call of the forbidden.

Misbehavior in life may not always be tolerated, but in art it often leads to innovation. I may still be compulsively polite in my day-to-day existence—quick with thank-you cards and phone calls home to the folks—but I can be rambunctious, irreverent, and even preposterous on the page. Literature is, I believe, a very safe cage for the beast within.

Whenever I find myself crippled by writer's block, there is one phrase that sparks my imagination. It makes, I think, a fitting close as you prepare to launch into these three early works. I owe it to that ingenious aesthete and demented carnival barker Salvador Dalí: *"Repulsion is the sentry that guards the gate to all that we most desire."*

DOUG WRIGHT
March 2005

Interrogating the Nude

AUTHOR'S NOTE

IN 1913, Americans caught their first glimpse of modern European art at the Armory Show in New York City. Picasso, Braque, and Brancusi were all represented in the exhibition. The unqualified "hit" of the show, however, was a painting by a little-known French artist named Marcel Duchamp. Its title was *Nude Descending a Staircase*, and it showed a cubist nude set in motion down a series of steps. Reaction to the painting ranged from ridicule to outright hostility. The public had never before seen the most sacred of art's subjects—the human form—treated with such irreverence. The show was picketed, riots broke out, and Theodore Roosevelt took a loud stance against the painting. Consequently, it sold for a handsome price. Duchamp became an instant celebrity in this country, and was later credited as the founder of the New York Dada movement. His reputation as dandy, philosopher, and enfant terrible of the art world eclipsed his reputation as an artist.

In exploring the genesis of Duchamp's notorious painting, this play disregards the biographical aspects of the artist's life in favor of his body of work: the art itself. Biographical data has been re-ordered to serve the plot, and many events are purely fictive, including the play's central metaphor, the murder of Rose Selavy. In short, the play hopes to capture the mystery, morbid whimsy, and sinister wit of Duchamp's world.

Interrogating the Nude was originally produced by the Yale Repertory Theatre (Benjamin Mordecai, managing director) in New Haven, Connecticut, on January 10, 1989. It was directed by Gitta Honegger; the set and costume design was by James A. Schuette; the lighting design was by Mark London; and the production stage manager was Joe McGuire. The cast was as follows:

THE DISTINGUISHED GENTLEMAN/
    CONSTABLE PUBLICK . . . . Peter Appel

MARCEL DUCHAMP . . . . Brad O'Hare

THE INSPECTOR . . . . Jerry Mayer

MAN RAY . . . . David Purdham

ROSE SELAVY . . . . Kirk Jackson

CHARACTERS

THE DISTINGUISHED GENTLEMAN

A renowned art historian. He wears thick glasses and is prone to overlong pauses when lecturing, which he does with droll pomposity.

MARCEL DUCHAMP

A slender man with delicate features, a dangerous wit, and a pronounced European flair. He has a cool exterior, with an impish glint in his eyes.

THE INSPECTOR

A hard-boiled gumshoe devoted to truth, the New York Police Department, and his three little girls.

CONSTABLE PUBLICK

An overworked, underpaid rookie who's more fond of gambling in the back room than he is of police work. The "Greek messenger" of the play.

MAN RAY

Swarthy and intense, with all the temperament that comes with artistry. He's most vulnerable when it comes to booze and sex.

ROSE SELAVY

A dark, wily creature of formidable passion. Fond of disguise, mystery, and deception, she has pale skin and a black soul.

TIME

It's 1913. The year of the Armory Show, the first major exhibition of modern European art in the New World. A time caught between

the lumbering grind of the Industrial Age and the permissiveness of
the Roaring Twenties.

NOTES FOR CASTING

The same actor may double in the roles of THE DISTINGUISHED
GENTLEMAN and CONSTABLE PUBLICK. In addition, the role of ROSE
SELAVY should be undertaken by a male actor, similar in build and
appearance to the actor cast as MARCEL DUCHAMP.

SETTING

The majority of the play takes place in a police precinct on the
West Side of Manhattan. The station occupies an isolated space
downstage. It may be illustrated by a few well-chosen properties: a
large, rough-hewn desk, a low-hanging interrogation bulb, and a
few stiff chairs. Amber hues spill across the floor, and the air is thick
with cigarette smoke. A ceiling fan might turn ominously, casting
shadows across the furniture.

During the play's first act, DUCHAMP may transform the areas
surrounding the precinct office into other locales by simply opening traps, drawing curtains, and magically introducing selective ob-
jects into the space. Like a ringmaster, he guides the action and
worlds of the murder story. He may re-create MAN RAY's apartment
by snapping his fingers, and thereby producing a clothesline dripping photographs, a camera atop a tripod, and a cot. His own studio might be suggested by an easel, a bottle rack, and a bicycle
wheel mounted on a stool. Large movie lights placed strategically
about the stage allow him to focus action as he chooses, in pools of
directed light.

In the second act, the prison cell may be indicated by bars, or a
gridlike pattern of yellow light. The locales should flow effortlessly

from one to the next, and the actors should move about the space with fluidity.

Far upstage, looming above the precinct office, is a large artist's canvas, rippling with the image of a reclining, classical nude. An imposing staircase rips through the canvas, and winds downward to meet the floor. Its steps are large and splintered, jutting out at uneven angles. It's clear that this climb is a perilous journey. The stairs broaden at the base, opening out to form the stage.

Prologue

(THE DISTINGUISHED GENTLEMAN *speaks in an authoritative voice from behind a podium.*)

THE DISTINGUISHED GENTLEMAN: Like the pilgrims who settled at Plymouth Rock and the gold miners who braved the untamed West, so, too, has the history of American art enjoyed its pioneers. Just as our forefathers washed upon the shore, Europe's dispossessed eager to forge cities in the uncharted landscape, foreign artists came to challenge our aesthetic terrain. One such artist was Marcel Duchamp. Although he grew up outside Paris, in a town as picturesque as any depicted by Monet, at the fledgling age of twenty-eight Duchamp packed his palette and sailed aboard the S.S. *Rochambeau*, arriving in New York on June 15, 1915.

A reticent intellectual who scorned undue attention, the genteel painter was as content playing chess in quiet repose or enjoying a well-blended tobacco in his signature pipe as he was unleashing new designs upon canvas. He was hardly prepared for his reception in the New World. His painting *Nude Descend-*

ing a Staircase, with its curiously disjointed form, angular composition, and altogether strikingly original portrayal of a nude caught in the act of descension, captured the whimsy of connoisseurs and the public alike, and established the young Duchamp as a major force in a country eager to make its own bold strides into art's future. Duchamp spent most of his life in New York, and eventually abandoned painting for philosophy. He died in 1968.

(DUCHAMP *enters on a bicycle. He stops, parks, and approaches the podium. From his pocket he pulls a small tin of black paint and a brush. As the lecture continues, he paints a goatee on* THE DISTINGUISHED GEN-TLEMAN's *face. When he has completed his work,* DUCHAMP *returns to his bicycle, mounts it, and pedals offstage.*)

After his death, his work was bequeathed to the Philadelphia Museum, where a special gallery now pays tribute to his invaluable contributions to a country forever bent on broadening its horizons.

(*Blackout.*)

ACT ONE

(Lights rise to reveal DUCHAMP *standing at the top of the stairs. To the strains of "La Vie en Rose," he lights his pipe and slowly descends. At the base of the stairs, he regards the audience for a moment, smiling.*

Next, he steps forward to confront THE INSPECTOR, *who sits behind his desk. Lights rise to a full glow in the precinct office.)*

DUCHAMP: Pardon, monsieur, I wish to report a crime.

INSPECTOR: Who doesn't? Have you filed a form?

DUCHAMP: A form?

INSPECTOR: Look, pal, it's a big city. Men get their pockets picked. Women get their purses snitched. Kids get their ice cream licked clean off the cone. So don't waltz in here boasting you've got some crime to report. You fill out a proper form, then you make an appointment, like the rest of 'em.

DUCHAMP: I'm afraid it's urgent.

INSPECTOR: Of course it is. They always are. What happened? Somebody lift your timepiece? Somebody spit on your shoes?

DUCHAMP: A woman's been dismembered.

INSPECTOR: What?

DUCHAMP: A nude woman, torn apart limb by limb, the pieces hurled down a staircase.

INSPECTOR *(Blanching.)*: My God . . .

DUCHAMP: Perhaps you have an appointment available this afternoon?

INSPECTOR: Don't get fresh with me, mister. If some poor girl's been butchered, that's serious business. Only how do I know you're on the up-and-up?

DUCHAMP: There's a leg on the landing.

INSPECTOR: Hmm. Yes. What say I file a report . . .

(The INSPECTOR pulls a thick stack of forms from his desk.)

You discover the body?

DUCHAMP: I did.

INSPECTOR: Your name.

DUCHAMP: Duchamp. Marcel Duchamp.

INSPECTOR: Come again?

DUCHAMP: D-U-C-H-A-M-P.

INSPECTOR: A foreigner, eh?

DUCHAMP: A Frenchman.

INSPECTOR: And what do you do for a living, er . . . ah . . .

(The INSPECTOR slips on DUCHAMP's name.)

. . . Mr. Doo-Champ? Don't tell me. Let me guess. Import, export. Wines, perfumes, ladies' undergarments and the like. I know you Frenchmen.

DUCHAMP: I am an artist, Inspector.

(The INSPECTOR makes a note.)

INSPECTOR: Unemployed. Any idea when the violence occurred?

DUCHAMP: Early morning. Half past one.

INSPECTOR: That's very good. Very exact. An eye for detail, eh, Mr. Doo-Champ?

DUCHAMP: The eye of an artist, Inspector.

INSPECTOR: We'll have our man in no time, won't we?

DUCHAMP: I expect we shall.

INSPECTOR: The scene of the crime.

DUCHAMP: Thirty-three West Sixty-seventh Street.

INSPECTOR: A residence?

DUCHAMP: Mine.

INSPECTOR: Is that so?

(Pause.)

I want to send a patrolman around to your place. You won't mind if he does a little poking around? Chalk on the floor, some dusting. Standard procedure.

(The INSPECTOR *calls for* CONSTABLE PUBLICK.*)*

Constable Publick, inside my office. Pronto!

(No answer. The INSPECTOR *questions* DUCHAMP *further.)*

Your apartment? Burglarized?

DUCHAMP: Nothing to take, monsieur.

INSPECTOR: Any telltale clues lying about the room?

DUCHAMP: All about. Arms, legs, feet, ribs, somersaulting down the steps . . .

INSPECTOR: No, goddamnit, I mean the weapon! The machete. The scythe. The hacksaw.

DUCHAMP: A palette knife and two paintbrushes. Camel hair.

*(*DUCHAMP *presents a small bundle to the* INSPECTOR.*)*

INSPECTOR: Nothing else? A hatchet, perhaps? Not even a lousy bread knife?

DUCHAMP: Wedged beneath the sofa, crumpled in a heap, I found these.

*(*DUCHAMP *holds forth another bundle.)*

A feathered hat and some old opera gloves.

(*The* INSPECTOR *takes the bundle and inspects the clothes. The gloves are black and beaded, and the hat is an explosion of dark feathers.*)

INSPECTOR: Hmm . . . Expensive fabric. Possibly imported. God-damnit, where is he? Constable! Get in here! Now!

PUBLICK (*From the wings.*): Aw, Chief, I got a helluva hand here!

INSPECTOR: You heard me!

(PUBLICK *enters, cards in hand.*)

PUBLICK: Chief, look! A full house. And I'm in hock up to my el-bows! Only thing I got left as collateral is my goddamn badge!

INSPECTOR: Remember your post, Constable. You're on assignment. This is Mr. Doo-Champ. Claims he witnessed a homicide around one-thirty in the a.m. I want you to verify his story. Round up the boys and visit this address. Inspect the premises for any disar-ray. Furniture topsy-turvy. Broken windows. Appendages.

PUBLICK: Ah-penda-what?

INSPECTOR: Who told you police work was pretty, Publick? You want a dainty job, paint pictures. Right, Mr. Doo-Champ?

DUCHAMP: Oh, quite right.

INSPECTOR: Report back to me with your findings. If necessary, no-tify the coroner.

PUBLICK: Dead dogs on trolley tracks. Squabbles in butcher shops. Explosions in orphanages. I get the dregs, you know that?

INSPECTOR: Take a bucket, just in case.

PUBLICK: I could've played the saxophone. I had the talent.

(PUBLICK *exits. He can be heard on his way out.*)

Cash in your chips, boys, we're on duty!

INSPECTOR: If there's a weapon to be found, he'll smell it out. Kid's got a nose like a bloodhound.

DUCHAMP: The killer used brute force.

INSPECTOR: Bare hands?

DUCHAMP: Without question.

INSPECTOR: You said the body was hacked to pieces. . . .

DUCHAMP: It was . . . fragmented.

INSPECTOR: What are you telling me, that a human being had the strength to tear limbs like drumsticks? Impossible.

DUCHAMP: I was there, Inspector.

INSPECTOR: You saw the assailant?

DUCHAMP: Oh, yes. Indeed.

INSPECTOR: With his bare hands, eh? Well, now. My, my. He must've been a mighty big thug. A giant, subhuman son of a bitch. Fire in his eyes, blood on his breath, and fists like cannonballs.

DUCHAMP: He was a slender man with a dapper profile and a pronounced European flair. Adored by a few bosom friends, and a well-kept mystery to the public at large.

INSPECTOR: That's our man?

DUCHAMP: That, Inspector, is he.

INSPECTOR: Doesn't sound like a homicidal mangler, if you ask me.

DUCHAMP: It's always the quiet ones in the end. The men you least suspect.

INSPECTOR: The eye of an artist, you say. Let's put that to the test, shall we? You say you saw the man. What was he wearing? His shoes—did they lace or buckle? Come on, now! Tell me. Were his fingernails clean?

DUCHAMP: Cordovans, tightly laced. Flecks of paint wedged beneath his nails. Slight, ethereal, and fond of good tobacco.

(DUCHAMP *pulls a pipe from his breast pocket and begins filling it from a pouch.*)

INSPECTOR: That so?

(*The* INSPECTOR *stares at* DUCHAMP *for a moment, then begins circling him slowly.*)

How tall would you say he was?

DUCHAMP: My height, I should say.

INSPECTOR: Is that right?

DUCHAMP: In these shoes.

INSPECTOR: Catch wind of the fella's voice? An accent, perhaps?

DUCHAMP: Decidedly Français.

INSPECTOR: That's downright chilling, isn't it?

DUCHAMP: Chilling.

(DUCHAMP *lights his pipe and begins to puff.*)

INSPECTOR: You're an artist, eh?

DUCHAMP: I confess. I am.

INSPECTOR: The tools of the trade, that would include . . .

DUCHAMP: A palette knife and some camel brushes.

INSPECTOR: Let me see your fingernails.

(DUCHAMP *thrusts out his hands.*)

I think, Mr. Doo-Champ, that we've found our man.

DUCHAMP: Yes, Inspector, I believe we have. Will you be notifying the papers, or should I?

(With amazing speed, the INSPECTOR *pushes* DUCHAMP *into a chair. There is an abrupt change of lighting; the interrogation bulb glows white-hot, and illuminates the two men while the surrounding stage is plunged into darkness. The* INSPECTOR *is hunched and sweaty;* DUCHAMP *shifts in his seat. It's as if the interrogation had been going on for hours.)*

INSPECTOR: I'll teach you to play games with the N.Y.P.D.! So you're a killer, are you?

DUCHAMP: Only when provoked, monsieur.

INSPECTOR: Let's start from the beginning. The night of the crime, you and the victim were alone together in your apartment. Correct?

DUCHAMP: Very much alone.

INSPECTOR: At approximately half past one you slit the victim's throat with the palette knife from beneath your easel, and then you proceeded to subdivide her.

DUCHAMP: Precisely.

INSPECTOR: With your bare hands.

DUCHAMP: Precisely.

INSPECTOR: That's hard to believe. You're a slight man.

DUCHAMP: Perhaps she was a slight woman, Inspector.

INSPECTOR: Who was she?

DUCHAMP: Ooh, a dangerous question . . .

INSPECTOR: Maybe you didn't know her name. Won't be the first time I've seen it happen. Rosy, nameless farm girl comes into the big city. She's got stars in her eyes, you've got bloodlust in yours. Poor girl winds up buried in a hat box. Wouldn't surprise me at all if you never even thought to ask after her name.

DUCHAMP: Eros is eros is a Rose.

INSPECTOR: Huh?

DUCHAMP: Rose. Her name was Rose.

INSPECTOR: She got a last name?

DUCHAMP: Selavy. Rose Selavy. *Eros, c'est la vie!*

INSPECTOR: French, was she?

DUCHAMP: Of course!

INSPECTOR: One of your own, eh? My God, buddy, you're a bona fide cannibal, aren't you? Now what, may I ask, was the little lady's profession?

DUCHAMP: My muse. My Mama Dada.

INSPECTOR: Come again?

DUCHAMP: An artist's model. She posed for me in my studio.

INSPECTOR: I've heard that one before. Model. Actress. Chanteuse. All means the same in the end. Five dollars and a cheap hotel. Just how did she pose, Mr. Doo-Champ?

DUCHAMP: With composure.

INSPECTOR: No, I mean . . . how? What did she wear . . . when she posed?

DUCHAMP: She was nude.

INSPECTOR: Of course. You're a healthy man, eh, Mr. Doo-Champ? And this Rose. She's a hearty woman. . . .

DUCHAMP: What are you suggesting?

INSPECTOR: Let me see if I got this down. She would stand at one end of the room, in the buff, *à la naturale*, naked under the eyes of God, and you would stand at the other, all by your lonesome, hidden behind an easel, twiddling your brush. Well?

DUCHAMP: I have a small apartment, Inspector. The easel and the bed, they are side by side.

INSPECTOR: Aha! Good. Thank you. So it is, in fact, fair to suggest that your relationship with Miss . . . er . . .

(The INSPECTOR trips on the name.)

. . . Sellavie extended beyond professional.

DUCHAMP: I suppose so.

INSPECTOR: Way beyond.

DUCHAMP: Perhaps.

INSPECTOR: That you were, in fact, party to certain acts, private acts, possibly even perversions.

DUCHAMP: Please, Inspector.

INSPECTOR: Painting's not your only pleasure, is it, Mr. Doo-Champ?

(DUCHAMP is silent.)

Come now. I'm a man's man. No need to be shy.

DUCHAMP: We fucked, Inspector, like machines. Together, grinding, pounding with the relentless tenacity of steam engines. The mice beneath the mattress would scurry for their very lives. Afterward, we would sleep for days, our bones gelatinous and our skins chafed, so great was our exhaustion. We would forget to eat for weeks at a time, until we noticed our ribs arching outward beneath our naked skin. Then we would refuel, only to continue our recklessness. Sometimes I would abandon my canvas and paint Rose, her lips a fiery slash and her nipples sunbursts. I would create landscapes on her belly, and portraits on each cheek of her great white ass. Now are you satisfied, Inspector?

INSPECTOR (*Scribbling madly.*): Great . . . white . . . ass . . .

(*The* INSPECTOR *pauses for a moment and rereads what he has written.*)

I can't put this filth in my report! I'd be discharged! . . . Sunbursts, eh?

DUCHAMP: Ablaze.

INSPECTOR: Those paintbrushes of yours should be burned. Profaning human flesh like that.

(*The* INSPECTOR *makes a few more hasty notes.*)

What about her family, eh? I've got to polish my brass and stand tall, and tell some poor parents that their sweet baby's been pulverized. Any of her people living in this country?

DUCHAMP: Only me.

INSPECTOR: Blood relatives, Mr. Doo-Champ.

DUCHAMP: Rose was my twin.

INSPECTOR: *What?*

DUCHAMP: We shared the same umbilical cord, Rose and I. For a while, it was feared we shared the same heart.

INSPECTOR: You and this Rose, this tart with the fire on her titties and the faces on her ass, you had the same father? The same mother?

DUCHAMP: We were joined at birth.

INSPECTOR: Sure, sure. Like dogs in jars at Coney Island.

DUCHAMP: Even in the womb, we cuddled. It was predestined, before we entered the world. What could be done, Inspector? Try and resist fate.

INSPECTOR: I shouldn't be listening to this pornography. I've got a wife and three little girls at home. Brother and sister; it's a fact?

DUCHAMP: Fact or fiction, that's your department, not mine.

INSPECTOR: This Rose. Did she pose for other artists, too?

DUCHAMP: I flattered myself that Rose and I were inseparable.

INSPECTOR: Were you?

DUCHAMP: Apparently not.

INSPECTOR: She double-crossed you, did she?

DUCHAMP: Rose would lick my eyelashes with the tip of her tongue and promise in a low voice to pose only for me. Only I was privy to every curve, every follicle. Only I could breathe her breath, taste her hollows, reproduce her form—

INSPECTOR: Answer the question.

DUCHAMP: Yes. She double-crossed me.

INSPECTOR: So there were other men.

DUCHAMP: One. Another artist. If she'd betrayed me with countless others, it would have been easier. Better her heart be splintered in a thousand shards than two equal halves.

INSPECTOR: Now this, ah, third party, was he—?

DUCHAMP: No relation.

INSPECTOR: Thank God! But you knew him. . . .

DUCHAMP: He's a photographer. Nudes are his specialty. "Nude-scapes," he calls them.

INSPECTOR: "Skintypes," I call them. He took nudie pictures of your twin sister?

DUCHAMP: Made me a cuckold. A clown.

INSPECTOR: And just what does this photographer do with these skintypes of his?

DUCHAMP: Many sell at fashionable galleries, at fashionable prices.

INSPECTOR: And the shots of your sister—he sold them to strangers?

DUCHAMP: The pictures of Rose are his private stock. He hoards them the way a greedy child stashes sweetmeats. I've heard he keeps them locked in a birdcage, beneath his bed.

INSPECTOR: So tell me. This pornographer, does he have a name?

DUCHAMP: He calls himself Man Ray.

INSPECTOR: An alias if ever I heard one. We'll need a description to track the son of a bitch down for testimony.

DUCHAMP: By day he's a man's man, swilling beer, wine, and whiskey in a single glass, spouting dirty stories in the middle of an arm wrestle.

INSPECTOR: But by night . . .

DUCHAMP: He fancies himself a ladies' man, going through models the way most artists go through paint, teasing them with his lens, then throwing them away like torn celluloid or spent cigarettes.

INSPECTOR: Or faded Roses, eh, Mr. Doo-Champ?

DUCHAMP: Some have a weakness for bonbons. Others for gadgets and automobiles. But Man Ray, impulsive and heedless, Man Ray had a *penchant pour la femme.*

(DUCHAMP *stands, steps away from the precinct office, and pulls open a trapdoor. A red light glows from beneath, suggesting a darkroom.*)

He once told me:

(MAN RAY *emerges from below.*)

MAN RAY: Christ, Duchamp, you've got me pegged all wrong. It's got nothing to do with lust. It's technique! To get a girl on film, I've got to know her body firsthand. Hell, Cézanne squeezed pears before sketching them, didn't he? It's symmetry. It's proportion. You understand. I use sex to compensate for a bad eye.

DUCHAMP *(To the* INSPECTOR.*)*: I'll never forget the night he confessed the hope that Rose might join his celluloid harem. It was well after midnight; we'd emptied a bottle of pirated booze and took turns sucking on it for flavor. He broached his scheme with due caution; his boorishness had driven all other prospects away.

(Lights rise on MAN RAY*'s apartment.* DUCHAMP *enters the space. While* MAN RAY *hangs fresh photos on the line,* DUCHAMP *fiddles with the pieces on a nearby chessboard.)*

MAN RAY: I've had it, Duchamp. The last straw.

DUCHAMP: What now?

MAN RAY: Look at me. Am I such an almighty, ever-loving *pig*?

DUCHAMP: Another model, flown?

MAN RAY: Bernice, the barmaid, works at the Pepper Pot. Two beers and a lobster dinner. I take her back to my place, pull out my camera, and you know what she says to me? "Portraits only, from the neck up!"

DUCHAMP: So?

MAN RAY: So, if I want headshots I'll snap my own! But I butter her up. "In a photograph," I tell her, "you can live forever. No wrinkles. No liver spots. Let me stitch you forever in the fabric of time."

DUCHAMP *(Aside, to the* INSPECTOR.*)*: Under duress, the photographer turns poet!

MAN RAY: Pearls before swine! "Listen here, ace," the tart starts shouting. "when I said I'd come back with you, I never promised a souvenir program!" I offer money—that really lights her fuse. "Oh, hooray! Mr. Vanderbilt! Quick, I'm gonna book myself a cruise!" She heads for the door. "In Paris," I say, "even aristocratic women are dying to pose. On their knees, they beg men like me."

DUCHAMP: And did she?

MAN RAY: *"Vive la France!"* she says, and slams the door.

DUCHAMP: You've been chasing nudes for months. Try something new.

MAN RAY: Like what? Bowls of fruit?

DUCHAMP: An apple or a melon might weather your insults better than a woman.

MAN RAY: I should photograph Rose.

DUCHAMP: Who?

MAN RAY: Your sister. Rose. She's been kicking around inside my head for weeks. You say she's exotic . . . that she bristles with mystery.

DUCHAMP: Rose—my Rose—in your apartment, on your couch, pinned beneath your camera? No. Why, it's absurd.

MAN RAY: Photographs. That's all I want from her.

DUCHAMP: I know you better than that.

MAN RAY: She's your sister! Private property. Look, if you'd feel safer, I'll tie my hands behind my back and pull the birdie with my teeth, eh?

DUCHAMP: You've never even seen her. She photographs poorly, I guarantee.

MAN RAY: She's your twin, isn't she? People give you the eye; I've seen it. Women, sure, but men, too. Your sister must be—how do you say it?—a femme fatale. So at least ask her. A little favor between friends. What's to lose?

DUCHAMP: Impossible. Even the suggestion is shocking . . . beyond remarkable. . . .

MAN RAY: Let her speak for herself. Who knows? She might like me. Some women have.

DUCHAMP: Rose has little in common with your downtown girls.

MAN RAY: I'm through with tarts, once and for all. All those big, lazy bodies dripping off stools. I want a woman with a mind to expose as well as a chassis! Push past the flesh to capture the subconscious! Let the camera penetrate the mysteries of the mind. Shoot what's inside a woman's head. What beats in her chest.

DUCHAMP: And Rose is your first candidate?

MAN RAY: Yes!

DUCHAMP: Pity.

MAN RAY: What do you mean?

DUCHAMP: She'll refuse, of course.

MAN RAY: How do you know?

DUCHAMP: Rose is private by nature. She would never put her dreams on exhibition.

MAN RAY: A thought passes across her forehead. A look. A gesture. *Snap!* I've got it on film. She'll never know what hit her.

DUCHAMP: Rose will know. She may turn the camera on you instead.

MAN RAY: Trust me. I can handle her.

DUCHAMP: You say you want to peel her apart. . . .

MAN RAY: In a photograph . . .

DUCHAMP: To expose her core . . .

MAN RAY: Landscapes of the mind . . .

DUCHAMP: Hmm . . . Fascinating!

(Pause.)

No. Absolutely not. Never.

MAN RAY: *Why the hell not?*

DUCHAMP: You'll thank me in the future.

MAN RAY: Don't be an ass! Just ask her. What harm could come of it?

DUCHAMP: Harm? What harm indeed . . .

(DUCHAMP breaks free from the scene and returns to the INSPECTOR. The lights in MAN RAY's apartment fade.)

INSPECTOR: This Man Ray fellow. Went behind your back, did he? Led your sister down the wayward path.

DUCHAMP: No, Inspector! It was she who approached him. A born strumpet, Rose. The secret trysts. The midnight assignations. She orchestrated them all.

INSPECTOR: All the while, pulling the wool over your eyes.

DUCHAMP: Oh, I knew, Inspector. I knew. In his apartment, in his studio, on backstreets. I was never far behind.

INSPECTOR: Hot on their trail, were you? An amateur detective? A Peeping Tom. Learned more than you bargained for, I'll hazard.

DUCHAMP: My suspicions were confirmed, my darkest fears made palpable.

INSPECTOR: Just what went on behind closed doors?

DUCHAMP: Why, Inspector. I'm surprised. Your wife and your three little girls . . .

INSPECTOR: I'm not here to tickle my jollies, Mr. Doo-Champ. I mean business.

DUCHAMP: Then prepare yourself. I'll spare no details.

INSPECTOR: By all means.

DUCHAMP: What follows may unnerve the faint of heart.

INSPECTOR: My heart's granite, Mr. Doo-Champ. Stone.

(*As* DUCHAMP *launches deeper into his confession, his voice rises in and out of fever pitch, his story a blend of farce and Grand Guignol. He draws a red silk curtain behind the* INSPECTOR's *desk. Translucent, behind the curtain,* ROSE *appears, alternating in the light between nudity and silhouette.* DUCHAMP *begins his litany, and* ROSE *follows instructions. The* INSPECTOR *watches with all the salacious enthusiasm of a peep-show devotee. "La Vie en Rose" wafts into the room.*)

DUCHAMP: I remember the night of their first meeting. I watched from the bed, feigning sleep, while Rose enacted her ritual. Composing herself before the mirror. The soft pink palette of Fragonard. Her Botticellian hips. Pivoting before the glass, tripling her reflection, like Raphael's Graces in a hedonistic dance. She peeled off her nightdress and the air caressed her shape. She powdered her body till the skin shone like bone, parched and smooth.

(ROSE *powders herself with an oversized puff.*)

She painted her lips violet. Violent violet.

(ROSE *applies lipstick.*)

Silk stockings like second skins.

(ROSE *slips on stockings.*)

She stepped into shoes with sloping heels and beady-eyed buttons.

(ROSE *steps into a pair of high-button black shoes.*)

Gloves to cover the hands that would tousle his hair and plow the furrows of his back.

(DUCHAMP *gingerly unfolds the gloves, which lie atop the* INSPECTOR's *desk. He fondles them gently as* ROSE *pulls on an identical pair that extend to her shoulders.*)

And then, a crown of magnificent plumage.

(DUCHAMP *considers the hat, while* ROSE *places the same hat on her head.*)

Ostrich and peacock feathers sprouted from her temples, swooping down in the back to bob at her waist. Finally, she slid into a cloak as black as her soul.

(ROSE *pulls on a stunning black cloak, dripping beads and bursts of vulture plumes. She admires herself, posing for the mirror.*)

At last the masking was complete. "Where are you going, *ma chérie?*" I called from beneath the covers.

(ROSE *pulls the red curtain aside and steps into full view.*)

ROSE: Out.

DUCHAMP: —she replied. With that, she crept from the apartment, confident that she'd left me behind. I hid in her shadow; our footfalls synchronized.

(ROSE *slips from the precinct office;* DUCHAMP *follows her. Together they slip in and out of darkness.* ROSE *casts furtive glances over her shoulder, and* DUCHAMP *quickly conceals himself in response. They play cat and mouse. The* INSPECTOR *watches every move.*)

Together we dodged the abandoned streets. Finally, she knocked on his door.

(They arrive at MAN RAY's *apartment.* MAN RAY *is asleep, tangled in sheets.* ROSE *pounds madly.* DUCHAMP *slinks into the shadows to observe.)*

I lodged myself beneath an open window, out of sight but not of sound.

*(*MAN RAY *tosses and turns.)*

MAN RAY: Oh God . . . Oh shit . . . Hey, Whoa, Shut up! Nobody's home! Get back on the streets where you belong!

*(*ROSE *pounds harder.)*

I'm too drunk, baby. And besides, I'm broke! Finis! Kaput! Try the Russian downstairs!

*(*MAN RAY *wraps stray bedding around his waist, then goes to the door. When he swings it open,* ROSE *wafts into the room.)*

ROSE: A gracious welcome, monsieur.

MAN RAY: Christ, I thought you were someone else. Who are you?

ROSE: Close the door.

MAN RAY: Are you lost? Big night on the town, too much juice— now you're all turned backward? You remember the name of the bellhop but not the hotel?

ROSE: You American men are all the same. Every woman you meet is a potential prostitute.

MAN RAY: Optimists, all of us. Look, ah, lady. Strangers don't usually drop by in the middle of the night.

ROSE: No? It sounds as though you are quite accustomed to strange ladies banging down your door. Turn out the lights.

MAN RAY: Do I know you? Have we met before?

*(*ROSE *turns out the lights. The moon spills across them.)*

Wait a goddamn minute! With all due respect, this is my apartment! You can't barge in here like a fucking locomotive!

ROSE: Shh! We'd better speak softly. I thought I heard someone behind me in the dark. There'll be trouble for us both if he discovers my whereabouts.

MAN RAY: Maybe you've got the wrong address.

ROSE: Don't toy with me, please.

(MAN RAY *opens the door and sticks his head outside.* DUCHAMP, *lurking in the shadows, skirts out of sight.*)

MAN RAY: Hello? Anybody there? Yoo-hoo! Hey, anybody lose a pretty lady with a big black hat—?

ROSE: Don't shout! You mustn't!

MAN RAY: All's clear. Street's empty.

ROSE: *Vive Dieu!* Perhaps it was the echo of my own footsteps.

(ROSE *tugs seductively at her garter.*)

MAN RAY: Miss, look at me, eh? I'm tired. I'm tanked. Hell, I'm wearing nothing but laundry. How 'bout we meet for breakfast instead—

ROSE: But you are Man Ray, no?

MAN RAY: How do you know my name?

ROSE: I know much more than your name, monsieur.

MAN RAY: Oh, my God. It's you, isn't it? He said you'd never come! He said it was impossible, you'd be insulted. . . .

ROSE: Marcel pretends to know who I am and what I want. That pesky little man is always putting words into my mouth.

MAN RAY: God knows what I expected, but I didn't expect—

ROSE: Rose disappoints you?

MAN RAY: I didn't say that.

(ROSE *heads for the door, ready to depart.*)

ROSE: Perhaps I am not the woman you hoped for. Perhaps your bottle is better company.

(MAN RAY *intercepts her.*)

MAN RAY: Don't go. Not yet.

(DUCHAMP *turns to the* INSPECTOR *and makes a remark.*)

DUCHAMP: They were attracted to each other with the pungency of alley cats.

MAN RAY: You came to pose?

ROSE: That depends, monsieur. If I consent to pose, what will I receive in return? Surely you don't expect me to sneak out of the apartment at absurd hours, incognito, and come all the way here in blinding cold only to shiver naked in front of machinery?

MAN RAY: Ah . . . what did you have in mind?

ROSE: Equitable treatment. The same attention you grant your other models.

MAN RAY: My other models all come from the Bowery. I could never treat a lady the way I treat a whore.

ROSE: Why not, if the lady prefers it?

MAN RAY: Then she's no lady.

(*Again,* DUCHAMP *makes an aside to the* INSPECTOR.)

DUCHAMP: Bravo, Man Ray! He'd hit the nail on the head!

MAN RAY: You've been here two minutes and already we're in hot water. Hell, Duchamp's my best friend. I swore up and down . . . I couldn't possibly.

ROSE: Ah! I see now. You're afraid of me.

MAN RAY: Don't be stupid.

ROSE: You've never been afraid of a woman before. They've always been afraid of you, yes?

MAN RAY: Nothing personal, but you move faster than sparks through wire.

ROSE: All I ask is to be kept warm.

MAN RAY: You understand, of course, that in my line of work indiscretion is an occupational hazard. It's not easy doing what I do. Arranging the model. Assessing every curve. It's true, I'm an artist, but I'm also a man. Every photograph I take is a triumph of mind over body. Of, ah . . . art over urge.

ROSE: It's what renders them provocative, monsieur.

MAN RAY: Just so I don't alarm you.

ROSE: *C'est impossible.*

(MAN RAY *ushers* ROSE *to the bed.*)

MAN RAY: Your charm's downright dangerous. It may melt the lens clean off my camera.

(ROSE *primps on the bed.*)

We'll begin with a simple portrait. Nothing racy, nothing rude. Now, if you'd be so kind—

(MAN RAY *adjusts his camera, then flips on a lamp to illuminate* ROSE's *face. He stares at her for a second, then recoils.*)

Oh fuck . . .

ROSE: My brother and I are bookends, are we not, monsieur?

MAN RAY: Bookends! I might as well seduce Duchamp.

ROSE: Prints from the same negative. I've been known to hide in my brother's profile.

MAN RAY: Let's forget the whole thing. Tonight never happened. Understood?

ROSE: Do you know what I risked coming to see you this way? You're not tossing me back onto the street!

MAN RAY: Think of Duchamp. He'd hate us both. We can't do that to him, can we?

ROSE: I'm not his property. I do as I please.

MAN RAY: It's no use! I look at you, but I see him!

ROSE: Perhaps you'd prefer his company. I've never seen two men so enamored of each other. Together at all hours, boozing, carousing. God knows how you pass the time.

MAN RAY: It's late. I'm warning you. Run along home.

ROSE: You're blushing!

(ROSE *swivels the camera to capture* MAN RAY'S *crimson expression, then dissolves into giggles.*)

MAN RAY: You're shameless!

ROSE: I'd envisioned you to be so many things, but a coward wasn't one of them.

MAN RAY: Is that a challenge?

ROSE: Perhaps you're only capable of shooting with your camera.

MAN RAY: Who else do you tease behind his back? The milkman in the morning? The postman in the afternoon?

ROSE: Tell me, does this pass for wit on the Bowery?

MAN RAY: How about the policeman on the corner when Duchamp ducks out for the evening paper? Or the dogs who come up the back stoop begging for soup bones?

ROSE: *Tu es un homme dégueulasse!*

MAN RAY: I won't be the first to pluck you, Rose!

(MAN RAY *climbs into the bed and plants a passionate kiss on* ROSE'S *lips. He loosens the sheet around his waist and, with a flourish, covers them both.* DUCHAMP *gasps and puts his head in his hands. The* INSPECTOR *rushes forward to halt the action.*)

INSPECTOR: That'll do! Yes. Thank you. That's sufficient. The gist of the matter, it's very clear.

(*Lights fade on* MAN RAY'S *apartment.*)

DUCHAMP: He violated every inch. He blackened every orifice. Then he photographed her for hours. Each fragment, each limb. Her backbone, her throat, her belly—a positively encyclopedic array. And he didn't stop there, Inspector. Oh, no. He photographed the two of them together, suspending his camera to immortalize their coupling. She never protested once.

INSPECTOR: Does this room seem warm to you? Look at me. I'm sweating like a pig.

(*The* INSPECTOR *offers* DUCHAMP *water from a pitcher on his desk.*)

Water?

DUCHAMP: *Merci.*

(*They drink.*)

INSPECTOR: So how long did the two of them continue to meet?

DUCHAMP: Days. Weeks. On into months.

INSPECTOR: And you knew all along?

DUCHAMP: Rose knew she could never deceive me. We shared the same breath, the same heartbeat. She did it to torture me, to prove her independence.

INSPECTOR: Why didn't you call the little lady's bluff?

DUCHAMP: I thought I could torture her by feigning indifference! I proved a poor actor.

INSPECTOR: Months of pent-up rage, disrupting the ebb and flow of the body's humors. Building to explosive levels. A walking time bomb, eh, Doo-Champ? Describe the moments that preceded her murder.

(DUCHAMP *stares at the* INSPECTOR *for a moment. The* INSPECTOR *coughs, then barks*).

Accuracy and detail, sir! Those are my interests!

DUCHAMP: It was late, almost midnight. I sat in one corner of the room, hunchbacked over my easel. Rose stood across from me. The moon spilled through the window and glazed us both. It was pagan, Inspector, in the extreme.

(DUCHAMP *swivels a nearby light to reveal* ROSE, *posing in a loose dressing gown. She stands astride a chaise longue, decked in pillows. An easel stands nearby.* DUCHAMP *enters the scene. Together they play the following sequence with melodramatic furor, occasionally glancing over shamelessly to gauge the* INSPECTOR's *response.*)

I dabbed, dipped, scraped, and stroked. I noticed how, with each passing minute, she grew restless, until at last she erupted, a full-blown symphony of nerves. Her toes tapped, her fists contracted, and her eyes darted back and forth like anxious little fish in big glass bowls. I could no longer paint her. She was flickering like a Vitagraph.

(DUCHAMP *turns on* ROSE.)

Still, goddamnit! Aha! See there! You're twitching! Why so fretful? Am I keeping you from something, Rose?

ROSE: At this hour? Yes, Marcel. From bed.

DUCHAMP: Whose?

ROSE: What are you suggesting?

DUCHAMP: I hear you unlatch the door in the middle of the night. I watch from the window as you skulk down the alley. Seems I'm tending a nocturnal Rose.

ROSE: Yes, Marcel, you've found me out! Every night at this hour I go down to the shipyards to visit the sailors. Goodness, is it after midnight? The crew will be frisky. They'll be eager to dock their vessels. Joe carries a heavy cargo, and Freddy is quite the rear admiral. That's what you want me to say, isn't it? Anything to justify your suspicions, to make your anger rightful.

(ROSE *adjusts the pillows on her chaise, then reclines. She tosses open her dressing gown, revealing her backside, à la Ingres's* Odalisque.)

DUCHAMP: I added a touch of bitumen to her joints and smeared her belly in pale ocher. My own body was primed, every fiber pulled taut. I could feel the veins encircling my heart like coiled wire. I contemplated Rose from the rear—the way her hair met her shoulders in tendrils, the small scoop of her back, the pink undersides of her kneecaps. I hated the very bones that slid up and down beneath her skin.

(DUCHAMP *reclines beside* ROSE *and spits his accusation in her ear.*)

You've been posing for him, haven't you?

ROSE: For who? Who are you talking about?

DUCHAMP: He's captured every wrinkle, every pore on film, hasn't he? Those photos hanging in his darkroom are flaps of your hide!

ROSE: Listen to yourself. It's revolting.

DUCHAMP: He never captures the whole, does he? No. Oh, no. He only photographs the pieces. A sloping neck. An ass. Arms that float. He chops you up with that canvas of his, doesn't he?

ROSE: Paint fumes have melted your brain.

DUCHAMP: Is the butcher waiting for you now? Is he blowing hot air on his lenses, polishing them with your discarded drawers?

ROSE: Tell your stories to the mirror. Don't waste your breath on me.

DUCHAMP: Are you too late? Have I kept you too long? Is he all alone with his birdie and nothing to shoot?

ROSE: *Stop it!*

DUCHAMP: How could you?

ROSE: God, yes, Marcel! That's all I am! Your empty-headed puppet, your porcelain Rose! And now Man Ray has stolen the strings!

DUCHAMP: So it's true. . . .

ROSE: I ran to him in the middle of the night and gave him every curve, every follicle. Da Vinci smile. Botticellian hips. With every flash of his camera, he locked me in time.

DUCHAMP: You're over there now, aren't you? Caged in his little black box. Scorched onto his film! He's got you dangling in his darkroom, staring at him from a thousand tiny frames—

ROSE: Yes! I've spawned myself a hundred times! Man Ray taught me how! Thanks to him, my soul has been squared! Now, Marcel, am I painting the proper picture?

DUCHAMP: He touched you, didn't he?

ROSE: Yes! Yes, he did! Look, Marcel! Here's where he kissed me! And oh—here is where his nails dug into my back! What else can I show you, hmm?

(DUCHAMP *lunges toward* ROSE *and attacks her.*)

DUCHAMP: I took her face in my palms, like wood in a vise waiting to be splintered. I circled her neck with my right arm, using my free hand to find the palette knife hidden in my smock. She let out a squeal, and in a spasm broke away and ran from the room. On the landing, I lunged after her, grabbing her ankle. She slid forward and together we tumbled down the steps, and then . . . Oh God, forgive me . . . I was upon her. . . .

(DUCHAMP *trembles for a moment, then breaks free.* ROSE *recedes into darkness.*)

I'm sorry. I can't go on.

INSPECTOR: Good Lord, don't stop now!

DUCHAMP: She . . . I . . . It . . . *No!*

INSPECTOR: Goddamnit, Frenchman, I need a full report! You can't stop short of the crime itself!

DUCHAMP: I've told you enough, Inspector. Deduce the rest!

INSPECTOR: What's the matter, Doo-Champ? Story frozen in your throat? The thought of your poor sister, all piecemeal, turning the carpet crimson—

DUCHAMP: Don't, please!

INSPECTOR: She's gone forever, erased, finished, thanks to you. Takes the wind out of your sails, doesn't it? *Doesn't it?*

DUCHAMP: Stop. I beg you.

INSPECTOR: Pity we can't turn back the clock, eh, Doo-Champ? Pity we can't *pick up the pieces?*

DUCHAMP: *Leave me alone!*

INSPECTOR: Can't finish what you started, can you? Last night, when you were tearing up the poor girl, it almost felt good, didn't it? *Didn't it?* Blood pumping. Muscles popping. Heat rising out of your pores. A new feeling, eh, Doo-Champ? Enough to turn a slight man into a giant?

DUCHAMP: Mon Dieu!

INSPECTOR: But this morning it hurts, doesn't it? This morning you're all alone. No more Rose. No more cheeky portraits. No more sunbursts. No one to blame but yourself. Funny thing about regret. Always arrives too late.

(DUCHAMP *picks up the feathered hat from the* INSPECTOR'*s desk. He strokes it gently. There is a long pause.*)

Sad son of a bitch. Railroaded your way in here for a reason. Carrying an ugly secret around for hours, weighing you down, breaking your back, making you crazy. Do yourself a favor. Lift the load. Out with it.

DUCHAMP: Swim about in my nightmare, sir, and I guarantee it will soak through your skin. However, if you insist—

INSPECTOR: I insist.

DUCHAMP (*Calmly.*): Very well. Rose kept wriggling in an effort to crawl down the stairs. Her skin turned to canvas beneath me, rough in texture and drawn tight, its surface crusted with ancient paint. With my palette knife, I carved out her da Vinci smile. A single quick motion ripping through cloth and, lo and behold, I'd severed her head.

(DUCHAMP *drops the hat. It lands on the floor.*)

I disarmed my Venus.

(DUCHAMP *takes the opera gloves from the* INSPECTOR'*s desk, unfolds them, and lets them billow to the floor.*)

With a loud creak, I tore apart her frames at each jointure.

(DUCHAMP *cracks a pencil in half for emphasis.*)

INSPECTOR: My God . . .

DUCHAMP: Her legs jerked back and forth and back and forth, like pendulums in manic tempo. Her hips swiveled joyously like gears set free. Like a marionette cut loose from its wire, her limbs fell willy-nilly into blackness. And that, Inspector, was that.

(The INSPECTOR *pauses, staring at* DUCHAMP *for a long time.)*

INSPECTOR: Monster.

DUCHAMP: You've heard the truth, Inspector. The mystery is solved. Now, I suggest you notify the papers. I'll be happy to receive interested reporters in my cell. The whole story, uncensored. I'm prepared to repeat it all.

INSPECTOR: The hell you will.

DUCHAMP: Please, Inspector, there isn't much time! Tomorrow's edition must go to press. You'll be wanting recognition for your outstanding efforts in this case, I'm sure.

INSPECTOR: If I had my way, Frenchman, you'd hang without a word.

*(*CONSTABLE PUBLICK *enters. He is carrying a large flat canvas.)*

PUBLICK: Yo, Chief. You positive you gave me the right address: 33 West Sixty-seventh?

INSPECTOR: Quick. What did you find?

PUBLICK: That's just it, sir. Nothing.

INSPECTOR: What?

PUBLICK: A few things, sure. A bicycle wheel. A snow shovel. A bottle rack.

INSPECTOR: That's it?

PUBLICK: And this. It's a painting of some kind. Me and the boys, we couldn't quite figure out what it's supposed to be.

*(*PUBLICK *holds the canvas up for the* INSPECTOR. *Until the close of the play, the painting is always held so that it faces upstage, concealed from the audience's view.)*

DUCHAMP: Constable, please! You have my life in your hands.

PUBLICK: Reilly said he thought it was a cello filled with dynamite. Magruder said it looked to him like a fire in a cardboard factory. Me, I just call it ugly.

INSPECTOR: Did you look for bloodstains, did you check under the floorboards, in the closets?

PUBLICK: I'm telling you, Chief, there was nothing. No appendages, not even a finger or a toenail. For this, I lost a full house.

INSPECTOR: Constable Publick, your job is riding on this case. Now, are you absolutely sure the place was clean?

PUBLICK: Come on, Chief. If there'd been a human head on the doorstep I think I would've noticed.

INSPECTOR: Goddamn you, Doo-Champ. What the hell are you trying to pull?

PUBLICK: Pardon me for saying it, Chief, but it looks like you've got another half-wit on your hands.

INSPECTOR: Nobody asked you, Publick.

PUBLICK: I mean it. Probably wandered in here from Bellevue, just aching to spill sick stories into somebody's ear.

INSPECTOR: And I'm the man idiot enough to listen, is that it?

PUBLICK: No offense meant, but it's happened before. Remember that crackpot from the pet shop on Park? Three victims, he said: Mabel, Mattie, and Moe. Said he'd strung 'em up with fishing wire in the basement under the store. You book him on three counts of murder, find out later they was all Pekinese. Outside, all around, true-blue crimes are being committed, and here we are busting our chops over some Joe who's knocking off pups in the cellar!

INSPECTOR: Do me a favor, Constable. Stick to your job, so I can do mine.

PUBLICK: But if the man's a loon—

DUCHAMP: What would I gain by telling lies? The motive for murder, it's clear, but the motive for spinning idle stories?

PUBLICK: I'm telling you, Chief, he'll make us look like morons.

INSPECTOR: But goddamnit, suppose he's telling the truth! Suppose the victim's here, somewhere in the city, buried in the park or stuffed in a suitcase? We sense a smirk at our expense, and we send him home, scot-free, the charges dropped. The man's confessed a crime and we've said, "No, thank you." Next week her head arrives by post in Des Moines. The week after, her feet in Fort Lee. How will we look then, Constable? Eh? I don't want her blood on my hands! This man is guilty until we prove him innocent! Understood?

PUBLICK: Yes, sir.

DUCHAMP: Who is more frightening, Inspector? The man who once in his lifetime commits a crime, or the man who dreams daily of committing a million crimes?

INSPECTOR: Listen, you. I want some hard-boiled evidence, and I want it now! Unless you can back up your ten-dollar boasts, I'm going to dismiss this case.

DUCHAMP: What would you like me to tell you, Inspector?

INSPECTOR: The truth, for Chrissake!

DUCHAMP: My truth, or your truth?

INSPECTOR: All right, you spindly little charlatan. I won't be made to look like a dolt. I've spent thirty years here at the N.Y.P.D., and I'm not bending over backward to satisfy the sordid fetishes of a foreign pervert! When I say hard-boiled, I mean hard-boiled!

DUCHAMP: The painting. I offer you my painting. Solid evidence, no? Canvas, a wooden frame—

INSPECTOR: What's your painting got to do with anything?

DUCHAMP: You wish to see the body of the victim? There it is.

PUBLICK: Aw, Chief, here he goes! Don't swallow the same bad egg twice!

DUCHAMP: All that remains of my precious Rose is now on that canvas.

INSPECTOR: What the hell are you talking about?

DUCHAMP: After I killed her, her body became my palette. I dipped my brush into her veins to find the crimson hues. The black tones I owe to the vitreous liquid of her eyes, which I split open like plums. To achieve the lighter shades, the yellow and the beige, I crushed her bone with mortar and pestle and ground the powder with the grease from her fat.

INSPECTOR: You smeared the victim all over that slab?

DUCHAMP: Rose is now in my oeuvre forever! The painting was born of her spirit. Listen, and you'll hear it breathe. . . .

PUBLICK: Chief, you're following him like a dog with a bone tied to the end of its nose! Don't you see, that's what he wants?

INSPECTOR: *The truth, you son of a bitch, the truth!*

DUCHAMP: Buried in the park. Stuffed in a suitcase. Lost in the post. That's what you'd like me to say, isn't it? That, you'd believe!

INSPECTOR: Go ahead. Make it difficult. Make it ugly. We're not leaving the room until the truth gets told.

(Silence. The INSPECTOR *stares at* DUCHAMP. DUCHAMP *looks straight ahead without flinching.* CONSTABLE PUBLICK *rocks back and forth on his heels. Seconds tick by.)*

PUBLICK: Yo, Chief.

INSPECTOR: Now what?

PUBLICK: One thing you should know. While I was there, in his apartment, Mr. Doo-Champ had a visitor. Fella nearly knocked me down, he was pounding so hard.

DUCHAMP: *Zut alors!*

PUBLICK: I open up the door and he starts shouting, "Where is he? Where the hell's Doo-Champ?" "Who wants to know?" I says back to him.

DUCHAMP: What did you tell him? Please . . .

PUBLICK: The truth, what else? I told him you were here, sipping tea with the New York Police Department. That's what I told him!

DUCHAMP: *Pourquoi lui? Pourquoi maintenant?*

INSPECTOR: Quiet, Frenchman! Publick! Did you get the man's name?

PUBLICK: He was down the stairs and out the door before I had the chance. A real suspicious character, Chief. I'll wager he wanted more than a cup of sugar.

(MAN RAY *bursts into the* INSPECTOR's *office. He spies* DUCHAMP *instantly.*)

MAN RAY: There you are! I've been up and down the whole West Side. Hey, sport, what the hell are you up to?

(DUCHAMP *turns away from* MAN RAY.)

INSPECTOR: Just one minute there, mister. You can't just bust in here! This is a highly confidential criminal interrogation. Make an appointment!

PUBLICK: Chief, it's him! He's the one!

INSPECTOR: Mr. Doo-Champ, do you know this man?

DUCHAMP: I've never seen him before in my life.

MAN RAY: *What?*

INSPECTOR: All right, you. Your name. For official police records.

MAN RAY: Man Ray. What's it to you?

INSPECTOR: You're the pornographer?

MAN RAY: Photographer!

INSPECTOR: Whatever! You're him?

DUCHAMP: Constable Publick, show this man to the door.

INSPECTOR: Don't move, Publick!

(*The* INSPECTOR *towers over* DUCHAMP *and places his billy club over* DUCHAMP's *throat.*)

Maybe Mr. Ray here knows where you stashed the body. Maybe that's why you don't want him interrupting our little tête-à-tête. How about that, eh?

MAN RAY: Body? What body? Whose body? For the love of Christ, what the fuck is going on?

INSPECTOR: Your friend here is under arrest for the murder of Miss Rose Sellavie.

MAN RAY: *What?*

DUCHAMP: It's true, Man Ray. Forgive me.

MAN RAY: That's rich! God, that's good. Tell me, Inspector. What was the weapon? Charcoal? A paintbrush?

INSPECTOR: Perhaps the pornographer knows too much!

MAN RAY: This is ludicrous!

INSPECTOR: Maybe. Maybe not. Husbands shoot their wives. Parents shoot their children. Twins shoot each other. Every night I go to bed sure I've seen it all. Every morning I rise to a world ripe with grisly possibilities.

MAN RAY: Christ, can't you feel your leg being pulled?

INSPECTOR: Murder is no laughing matter! He's already confessed to the charge. What the hell. We'll lock him up.

DUCHAMP: Man Ray, please. You had no business finding me here. Get out. Go home. Leave us alone.

MAN RAY: Duchamp, listen to me. A game's a game, but you're playing with fire. These bumblers swallow your story, they'll lock you away for life.

DUCHAMP: Go. Please. It's the last favor I'll ever ask of you.

INSPECTOR: Nobody leaves!

MAN RAY: I'm telling you, Inspector, it's all a hoax!

INSPECTOR: Look at them, Constable. They're both raving.

MAN RAY: *There's been no murder!*

DUCHAMP: Don't, Man Ray! You mustn't! Please!

MAN RAY: Rose Selavy is alive and well!

(Blackout, fast.)

ACT TWO

(Seconds have elapsed since the close of Act One. The INSPECTOR, CON-STABLE PUBLICK, MAN RAY, *and* DUCHAMP *are all still assembled.)*

INSPECTOR: What? Rose Sellavie still alive? How can that be?

MAN RAY: He's a milquetoast, a pussycat. He'd kill himself before he'd ever lay a finger on Rose.

DUCHAMP: Lies, all lies. She's dead and gone. Her body's exploded outward in a symphony of color. She's dancing in the clouds above us, Inspector, lilting with the music of shattered violins!

MAN RAY: I know him; he's all talk! A lot of gory stories, sure, but inside he's gentle as a lamb. Just look at him, for Chrissake! Look at those hands. They're soft. White. Hairless. They're designed to hold paintbrushes, not knives or pistols! And what about that face, I ask you! You call that a killer's mug? No! A dandy, maybe, but never a crook.

DUCHAMP: Who is more cunning? The criminal who kills with a knife or the dandy who kills with a glance?

MAN RAY: What proof have you got of the crime? Any physical evidence? Anything at all?

DUCHAMP: They've confiscated my painting. What more do they need?

INSPECTOR: A victim, that's what we need!

PUBLICK: Apartment's clean. I'll stake a fiver on it.

MAN RAY: Don't believe a word he tells you. He makes a living off his fantasies. Never trust an artist, Inspector.

INSPECTOR: Just what do you call yourself?

MAN RAY: A photographer. I don't invent pictures, I capture the truth!

DUCHAMP: My God, Inspector! Is the world so corrupt that a man can't even confess his own crimes? Does the burden of proof now fall on the criminal? What must I do? Must I offer her remains on a plate? Her digits festooned?

INSPECTOR: An elbow or a kneecap might lend a little credibility to your story, Frenchman.

DUCHAMP: I'm warning you, I won't keep quiet. I'll go straight to the papers. Try withholding my story then, and see how the citizens turn against you. They'll storm the station. Men armed with baseball bats. Women brandishing rolling pins. People don't like being duped when they're in danger.

MAN RAY: By all means, Inspector. Host a party for the press. Announce a murder that never happened. Terrify the whole damn city. Then see how they thank you once they learn the truth.

INSPECTOR: Damn you, Mr. Ray. What makes you think you're any better than he is? Violating young ladies and recording it on film. The way I see it, you're both degenerates. You storm in here bellowing, "She's alive! Alive and well!" What brilliant piece of evidence have you put on the table, eh?

DUCHAMP: Bravo! Bravo, Inspector!

INSPECTOR (*To* DUCHAMP.): Another peep out of you and I'll string you up in my own backyard. (*To* MAN RAY.) Answer me. What proof do you have that Rose Sellavie still breathes with the best of us?

MAN RAY: Let me speak to you in private.

DUCHAMP: It's a trick, Inspector!

INSPECTOR: Snuff it, Frenchman!

DUCHAMP: But this is an official police interrogation! This man is lampooning it with his cheap theatrics!

MAN RAY: *My* cheap theatrics? That's the pot calling the kettle black!

INSPECTOR: Enough! Constable Publick, I think we'd better give Mr. Doo-Champ here a chance to cool off. I'd like to speak to Mr. Ray alone.

PUBLICK: A pleasure, Chief.

(CONSTABLE PUBLICK *seizes* DUCHAMP.)

DUCHAMP: Take your knobby little fists off me.

PUBLICK: Thataway, here we go. Upsy-daisy.

(*The* CONSTABLE *pulls* DUCHAMP *toward the door.* MAN RAY *rushes after him.*)

MAN RAY: I'm warning you, sport. You've pushed the limit with this gag. I'm only here to save your skin. I'm not here to play along.

DUCHAMP: The moment before her death she tried to call out your name, so I tore out her tongue.

MAN RAY: Why, you puny little savage—

INSPECTOR: Another word and I'll shoot!

(PUBLICK *drags* DUCHAMP *away.*)

A man strolls in here with his confession on a silver platter. Offers up everything but the one piece of evidence we need most. The body! Why? Without it, his claims don't hold piss.

MAN RAY: I'm telling you, it's a false alarm! You've been had, Inspector! There's no body. There's nothing. It's one big joke! Sick, sure, but that's his humor. The man's a walking circus. As long as you keep jumping through hoops, he'll keep tossing them in your direction.

INSPECTOR: Ever been the victim of a crime, Mr. Ray?

MAN RAY: You're the victim here, not Rose!

INSPECTOR: Ever seen a body gunned down in the heat of passion? Ever been down to the county morgue and peered under the sheets?

MAN RAY: Of course not!

INSPECTOR: Well, I have, and it keeps me awake nights, believe me. Clinging to the bedposts, listening to my heartbeat. Crime's not the stuff of comedy!

MAN RAY: Hell no. Crime's food on your table. It's a roof over your head. But to Duchamp it's a good guffaw.

INSPECTOR: Nobody here is laughing, Mr. Ray. That man is hiding something. Something big.

MAN RAY: It's a publicity stunt, that's all. When it comes to the tabloids, he'd stand on his head and paint with his prick, I guarantee.

INSPECTOR: But would he falsify murder?

MAN RAY: Why not? Men test the limits of the law every day to forward their careers. Lawyers, bankers, politicians. Why should an artist behave differently?

INSPECTOR: One thing's clear. He'll never get famous off his painting. I'd sooner let a monkey paint my portrait. A blind monkey with four broken hands.

MAN RAY: You're a policeman. You don't know art from your ass.

INSPECTOR: Don't talk to me about asses and art. Just what do you photograph? Landmark architecture?

MAN RAY: What do you hang up on the wall, other than your hat?

INSPECTOR: I'd sooner hang my hat than that jigsaw nude!

MAN RAY: You couldn't tell a decent painting from a third-rate bill-board!

INSPECTOR: I don't know much about art, but I do know this: here, we like our models clothed and in one piece.

MAN RAY: Fat ladies and fruit bowls. Weather-beaten barns, standing in wheat. I can guess your taste, Inspector.

INSPECTOR: I'll take an artist who knows the difference between anatomy and geometry, Mr. Ray!

MAN RAY: What's a painting to you, eh? Something to fill up a wall without windows?

INSPECTOR: Me, I got paintings all over the house! Daffodils and dogs and refined folks in velvet. You know why? Because there are cracks in the plaster, that's why! I'd sooner look at flowers than at water spots. Now, this work of his. This naked puppet. Why the hell would any God-fearing American hang one eyesore to cover up another? Eh? *Eh?*

MAN RAY: You want the goods on Duchamp or don't you?

INSPECTOR: That's what we're here for, isn't it?

MAN RAY: A ten-month show at a fancy Paris gallery, and he couldn't sell a single goddamn painting.

INSPECTOR: That's one helluva surprise. Can a grocer sell rotten fruit? Can a baker sell burned bread?

MAN RAY: You want the dirt or don't you?

INSPECTOR: Shoot.

MAN RAY: Overseas, competition's thick, and Duchamp was pitted against a tough crowd. This Spanish heavy named Pablo and his three henchmen: Brancusi, Braque, and Boccioni. Together they'd glutted the market. People, pipes, guitars—they'd all been shot through the prism. When revolution's in fashion, what's the point? Here in New York he thought his luck might turn.

INSPECTOR: In America, it's open season? Asylum for every half-cracked looney with a paintbrush in his hand? I hate to disappoint the fella, but here we know the value of our dollar!

MAN RAY: But suppose his painting was connected to a headline crime. A portrait of the victim. Her only remains. Buy the painting and you'd buy a chunk of history. Edge your way onto the front page.

INSPECTOR: This painting of his. It's gonna hang? In public?

MAN RAY: At the Armory Show, down on Twenty-sixth Street. This story hits the press and it's as good as sold. Three, maybe four hundred bucks.

INSPECTOR: All this hoopla over a two-bit picture painted by a charlatan? An artsy-fartsy freak show? For this he'd drag his sister through the mire?

MAN RAY: Worse. He'll drag you right along with her.

INSPECTOR: Not on your life.

MAN RAY: Just wait. Weeks pass, you can't deliver a corpse—you'll look like a buffoon. You'll be washed up. Not even fit for the dog catcher.

(The INSPECTOR's brow creases. He ponders this for a moment. MAN RAY leans in and whispers into his ear, building an ugly scenario.)

I can hear them now . . . the Constable and his rookie buddies snickering in the back room, taking bets over your job. You married?

(The INSPECTOR nods.)

Your better half, crying every night into her pillow, tears of shame . . . Children?

(The INSPECTOR *holds up three fingers.)*

Aw, Christ! I don't envy their time in the schoolyard. Their father, a laughing stock. Their little pinafores muddy with the dirt of your once-good name. . . .

(The INSPECTOR *can't take it any longer; his forehead streams sweat, and his bulging cheeks are about to explode. He bolts up and shouts in the direction of* DUCHAMP*'s cell.)*

INSPECTOR: *Why, that no good skinny little shit!*

MAN RAY: Don't get mad, Inspector. Get even. Hold him here a week, maybe two, behind bars. That way, his story won't leak to the press. The whole affair will blow over without a word.

INSPECTOR: I'll teach him the high price of low pranks. Let him stew a few days, eh? Bread and water. Maybe a coupla hours in the ice house.

MAN RAY: Inspector, I misjudged you. Why, you're sharp as a razor. Make sure he learns his lesson. Now, if you don't mind, I'm going home to bed. It's not even noon.

INSPECTOR: Oh, no you don't! You're not leaving this station!

(The INSPECTOR *pushes* MAN RAY *into a chair, and the interrogation bulb burns once again.)*

MAN RAY: What the hell . . . you can't . . . shit!

INSPECTOR: I'm placing you in police custody.

MAN RAY: I came to set the record straight! You almost made an ass out of yourself before the whole precinct!

INSPECTOR: Don't get in a conniption. One person holds the key to this case. I'd like her to confirm your story.

MAN RAY: You don't mean . . . no . . . no, that's impossible.

INSPECTOR: We'll let the victim speak for herself!

MAN RAY: Oh God . . .

INSPECTOR: Getting hot and bothered, eh? What's the matter now?

MAN RAY: Don't drag Rose into this mess. She's a fragile lady. She'll melt under the heat, I know it!

INSPECTOR: All she has to do is show herself and you're home free.

MAN RAY: You'll never find her.

INSPECTOR: Why not?

MAN RAY: You don't know where to look.

INSPECTOR: She sounds recognizable enough. Don't play innocent with me. I know every lurid detail, from the first leer to the final thrust.

MAN RAY: Duchamp told you . . . he said that Rose and I . . . Ha! He sure paints some bold pictures, doesn't he?

INSPECTOR: Come clean. Where is she?

MAN RAY: I haven't got a clue.

INSPECTOR: Bullshit.

MAN RAY: She's gone into hiding.

INSPECTOR: How do you know?

MAN RAY: A letter. This morning Rose slipped a letter under my door.

INSPECTOR: Why didn't you say so before? Hand it over, quickly. Let's have a look.

MAN RAY: No! I mean, I can't. Shit. I don't have it.

INSPECTOR: That letter may be your ticket to freedom.

MAN RAY: Give me half an hour. I'll dash over to my place and come back, letter in hand.

INSPECTOR: Don't insult me, Mr. Ray. You stay put, where you belong. I'll send the Constable. He'll rifle it down. Where'd you stash it? Well? Speak up, Mr. Ray. I can't hear you.

(MAN RAY *pulls a letter from his jacket.*)

MAN RAY: What luck! Right here, in my pocket. Christ, I feel like a fool.

INSPECTOR: How convenient. Give it here.

MAN RAY: No, I can't do that. This letter, it's highly personal. In fact, it's embarrassing. Rose would have my head.

INSPECTOR: I'll have your head if you don't give it here.

(The INSPECTOR *lunges for the letter.*)

MAN RAY: No! Goddamnit, Inspector! Have some respect for a man's privacy. If you don't mind, I'll read it to you.

(MAN RAY *unfolds the letter. Lights rise on a landing halfway up the stairs.* ROSE *begins reading.*)

ROSE: *Mon Cher:* We've been found out! The weasel accused me of an affair. Last night, while I was posing for him, he attacked me with his palette knife. It's no longer safe for me here. I've decided to disappear until his temper cools. I cannot tell you where I am, or how long I will remain. Rest assured that I am safe. My poor Man Ray. My poor, poor Marcel. You loved each other like brothers, and now I've splintered you apart!

MAN RAY: I'd prefer to skip this next part.

INSPECTOR: Read!

ROSE: Goodbye, Man Ray. When I sleep, I'll crease my pillow, and in my dreams thrust my lips between your flanks.

(ROSE *smiles, inserts the letter into the envelope, and licks its edges. She kisses the outside of the note.*)

Rose.

(ROSE *fades into darkness.*)

INSPECTOR: Downright primal, isn't she?

MAN RAY: The fact is she's gone. It's pointless to go looking.

INSPECTOR: Hand over that note. It's hereby property of the N.Y.P.D.

MAN RAY: No go, Inspector!

(*The* INSPECTOR *lunges again.* MAN RAY *shreds the paper and stuffs it into his mouth. The* INSPECTOR *encircles* MAN RAY'*s neck with his right arm, and twists* MAN RAY'*s left arm behind the back of the chair with his free hand. He holds him for a moment. Strips of paper protrude from* MAN RAY'*s mouth.*)

INSPECTOR: Publick! Get in here! Now!

(PUBLICK *enters, cards in hand.*)

PUBLICK: Here, sir!

INSPECTOR: If he so much as blinks, Constable.

(PUBLICK *aims his pistol at* MAN RAY. *The* INSPECTOR *loosens his grip and handcuffs the photographer. He pulls the tattered letter from* MAN RAY'*s mouth and inspects the soggy remains.*)

I suspected as much. An overdue bill for photographic supplies. I suggest you pay it.

(*He dumps the bill into* MAN RAY'*s lap.*)

MAN RAY: I burned the letter.

INSPECTOR: There is no letter. There never was. A final, flimsy stab at concealing the true crime. She's dead all right, and you had a hand in her killing.

MAN RAY: *What?*

INSPECTOR: Pieces all fit. Touching, really. Doo-Champ takes the rap to protect you. Comes in unbeknownst, spills his guts, claims he's killed her all by his lonesome. You protect Doo-Champ, screaming she's still alive, improvising phony letters.

MAN RAY: Why would the two of us want Rose on ice?

INSPECTOR: Colleagues. Soul mates. Blood brothers. You share the same crackpot notions, the same artistic mumbo jumbo. Maybe Rose had your number. Maybe she knew too much.

MAN RAY: About what?

INSPECTOR: Scoundrels able to scoff at murder must be guilty of greater crimes themselves.

MAN RAY: Rose isn't some tart, plucked off the Bowery! She's the man's sister!

INSPECTOR: Rape your sister and I'll hazard to say you could kill her as well. Admit it. There's a stiff, blue body collecting dust in your apartment. You don't want the Constable rooting around for fear he'll find it. Well, the game's over. What's your address?

MAN RAY: None of your goddamn business.

INSPECTOR: Hear that, Publick? He knows he's cooked.

MAN RAY: Forty-second Street, across from the station.

PUBLICK: On my way, Chief.

INSPECTOR: Break down the door if you have to.

MAN RAY: Do me a favor, Constable. Keep the hell out of my dark-room.

(*The* INSPECTOR *and the* CONSTABLE *smile knowingly at each other.*)

Open the door and you'll bleach all my prints! Photographs, that's all you'll find!

PUBLICK: Dirty pictures, Chief, whaddaya bet? Back in a jiff.

(PUBLICK *exits.*)

MAN RAY: He's done it, goddamn him. Wrapped us all up in the palm of his hand.

(The INSPECTOR *frees* MAN RAY *from the chair.)*

INSPECTOR: Stand up. Hands over your head. Face front. Follow me, you little photophile.

(The INSPECTOR *escorts* MAN RAY *across the stage and into the prison cell.* DUCHAMP *sits on a cot.)*

Meet your cellmate, Mr. Ray.

*(*DUCHAMP *and* MAN RAY *don't acknowledge each other in the* INSPECTOR*'s presence.)*

Now, you two bastards behave yourselves. You aren't dealing with amateurs. Constable Publick and I are trained to contend with the blackest of hearts. Rapists, pimps, cardsharks, thieves. Even con artistes like yourselves.

(The INSPECTOR *grins and exits.)*

MAN RAY: You're digging a grave deep enough for both of us. I hope you know that.

DUCHAMP: No one asked you to come. You blustered in here of your own accord.

MAN RAY: I hope this joke has one helluva punch line, 'cause so far I don't get it.

DUCHAMP: "Joke," Man Ray?

MAN RAY: You've got that poor oaf out there tripping over his own gumshoes. And he's not laughing, Duchamp. He's got steam coming out his ears!

DUCHAMP: The law is the law, yes? And when you're a civilized person, and you have broken the law, what do you do? Confess, of course.

MAN RAY: The Constable's ransacking my apartment right now, certain he'll find a body!

DUCHAMP: He won't. He never will.

MAN RAY: It doesn't matter! The next time a landlord finds bones in his furnace, or a leg washes up in the East River, they'll pin it on us!

DUCHAMP: Quiet. You'll give him ideas.

MAN RAY: Art and crime, they don't tango. Shit, I never thought I'd see the day when a mixed metaphor could land a man behind bars.

DUCHAMP: What did you tell the Inspector?

MAN RAY: That you're after a few headlines. You want your painting reproduced in the paper, so it sells. That's how you'll be remembered, sport. A con man who was short on cash.

DUCHAMP: What does it matter, eh? History reinvents us all.

MAN RAY: So what have you done with Rose?

DUCHAMP: Ah! *Ma petite fleur!* The little blossom, she has dropped off the vine.

MAN RAY: Well, the "little blossom" is due at my studio at midnight tonight! In full bloom, right down to her skivvies. A deal is a deal.

DUCHAMP: I can't. She can't. *We* can't.

MAN RAY: But I bought her a present. I was hoping she'd wear it at tonight's sitting. It's a mink stole with a genuine diamond clasp.

DUCHAMP: You shouldn't have.

MAN RAY: I didn't. It's rabbit with rhinestones, but in a photograph who can tell for sure?

DUCHAMP: Indeed. In a photograph things aren't always what they seem.

MAN RAY: So whaddaya say? Can I expect her?

DUCHAMP: No.

MAN RAY: Come on. I know Rose. The witching hour strikes and she'll be dying to take to the streets.

DUCHAMP: Her days of hide-and-seek are through.

MAN RAY: You wanna put money on that?

DUCHAMP: I can do many things, Man Ray, but I cannot raise the dead.

MAN RAY: Stop jerking me around, Duchamp!

DUCHAMP: It's best that it happened this way. Without warning, in a spasm of passion. It would be unbearable for you to see Rose and know it was for the last time. You'd be devastated. You'd smash your camera.

MAN RAY: You owe me!

DUCHAMP (*Definitively.*): I am not playing make-believe, Man Ray. The deed is done.

MAN RAY: You're . . . you're not bluffing?

DUCHAMP: Decidedly, no.

MAN RAY: But she's your muse. How will you keep painting?

DUCHAMP: I'll find a new subject. The time for sluggish nudes, rotting poultry, and dormant pears has passed. I'll paint engines— glistening oil, their levers erect and their cogs red-hot.

MAN RAY: What about me, eh? I finally find the perfect model, a woman unlike any other, and what happens? My best friend offs the lady!

DUCHAMP: The time had come. She gave birth to your photographs and to my painting. That's enough, isn't it?

MAN RAY: But you should see these prints! They're phenomenal! They're more than just portraits. They're X-rays of the soul. Her image leaps off the page and burns itself onto your eyes! I've captured shots of something private, something never before revealed on film. A fantasy. A piece of the mind! Beyond naked. Beyond nude. A secret, utterly and completely exposed. I can't let her go. I won't let her go. Not now.

DUCHAMP: You have no choice.

MAN RAY: A parting shot, eh? At least give me that.

DUCHAMP: No.

MAN RAY: Why not?

DUCHAMP: She's lived between us long enough. Alone in my head, what was she? An amusing fancy. A whim. After I introduced her to you, what was she then? A shared secret, nothing more. It's time we let the world take her.

MAN RAY: How can it, if you've killed her?

DUCHAMP: Try creating one thing without killing something else. What are your photographs but thin memorials to moments long dead? When Rose was invisible, she was ripe with possibility. Once you trapped her in your camera, she was done for. Certain face, certain hair, certain hat . . . certain death.

MAN RAY: So that's it. We've lost her.

DUCHAMP: No! Not at all. Not if her murder is headline fare! The whole world will remember her, experience her, read about her in the paper, overhear on the stoop: "Rose Selavy—why yes, she passed here every morning!" or "I saw her that night, walking toward his apartment, toward certain death. . . ." If the world gives Rose a place in its memory, then what has she become?

MAN RAY: A work of art?

DUCHAMP: Precisely!

MAN RAY: But most art is kept in frames, pal! On the wall!

DUCHAMP: Art belongs in cages, Man Ray? Confined for our amusement, bolted to the wall like a prisoner shackled to his torture rack? God forbid it should yank itself free, step into the third dimension, and start breathing! God forbid it should wander the sidewalks, stroll in and out of buildings, or, worse still, swing open the heavy door of a police station, yes?

(Pause.)

MAN RAY: God, sport.

DUCHAMP: Hmm?

MAN RAY *(Smiling.)*: I'll miss her.

(DUCHAMP puts an arm around MAN RAY's shoulder in mock sympathy.)

DUCHAMP: *C'est la vie!*

(The lights fade on the prison cell and rise on the precinct office. The IN-SPECTOR sits at his desk. PUBLICK enters. He is carrying a small square birdcage made from wire. It is filled with photographs. PUBLICK hurries to the INSPECTOR's desk.)

INSPECTOR: Over here, Publick, on the double!

PUBLICK: Bad news, Chief. Place was clean.

INSPECTOR: Not again!

PUBLICK: A camera, a tripod, a bed—nothing else.

INSPECTOR: What about the darkroom?

PUBLICK: Geez, you wouldn't believe it! Gams, elbows, faces, bellies all hanging off a clothesline. Downright eerie, I call it.

INSPECTOR: But no body?

PUBLICK: Nah. Only pictures.

INSPECTOR: What the hell have they done with her? Is she clogging the plumbing, or nourishing plants?

PUBLICK: Did find this, though, under the bed. Looks like a birdcage. It's got her name carved in the base. Good for fingerprints at least.

INSPECTOR: Better than that, Constable! You've found his private stash. His little box of nasties.

PUBLICK: Shall I have a look-see?

INSPECTOR: Keep your pants on, Constable. Our interest in these photographs is purely professional.

(The INSPECTOR *takes the birdcage from the* CONSTABLE *and sets it on his desk. He opens the door and withdraws the photographs. The* CONSTABLE *peers over the* INSPECTOR*'s shoulder throughout. The* INSPECTOR *stares at the first photograph.)*

PUBLICK: Got to watch out with a girl like that, Chief. Too hot for her own good. I'll bet when she kisses, it blisters.

INSPECTOR: Small wonder she drove two men to murder. Haunting, eh, Publick? His twin all right, no question. Same lofty brow . . .

PUBLICK: Same smirk, only lipsticked . . .

INSPECTOR: Same rigid nose . . .

PUBLICK: Same eyes, too, like they was looking past your body all the way to your shadow . . .

INSPECTOR: Same hands, tapering at the tips . . .

PUBLICK: Selfsame bones in his cheeks . . .

INSPECTOR: Same chin . . .

*(*PUBLICK *blanches.)*

PUBLICK: Yo, Chief! You don't suppose—

INSPECTOR: Hmm? What?

PUBLICK: Nah, forget it. My wife, she's always telling me I got a dirty mind.

INSPECTOR: Say it, Publick! What's on your mind?

PUBLICK: Without the hat . . . without the gloves . . . take 'em away, Chief, and what are you left with?

(The INSPECTOR *considers this for a moment. He tears a photograph, removing the top portion, presumably the hat. He then tears along the bottom, presumably removing the gloves. He stares at the torn image in his hand.)*

INSPECTOR: That's impossible. It's preposterous. Worse, it's obscene!

PUBLICK: Got to learn to keep my mouth shut, that's all.

INSPECTOR: It's the answer! By God, Publick, you've hit on it!

PUBLICK: Nah, you're bluffing. You're making fun.

INSPECTOR: Rose with her skirts hiked is no Rose at all!

(The INSPECTOR *collapses backward into his chair.)*

Constable, water!

*(*PUBLICK *pours a glass of water for the* INSPECTOR, *who downs it in a single gulp.)*

PUBLICK: Jesus, Mary, and Joseph! Spit on 'em, Chief!

*(*PUBLICK *spits on the photographs.)*

INSPECTOR: Bring 'em here. Bring 'em now. The time has come at last, Publick. I want to see them both exposed.

(Lights rise on the prison cell. PUBLICK *approaches.)*

PUBLICK: Follow me. Bring your dancing shoes. You've got some fancy footwork ahead of youse.

(DUCHAMP *and* MAN RAY *exchange a look.* PUBLICK *escorts them into the precinct office.*)

MAN RAY: You caught us red-handed, Inspector. Murderers, both of us. Duchamp's got his paintbrush, and I've got my lens.

DUCHAMP: New York is not safe.

MAN RAY: Not till we hang.

INSPECTOR: In galleries, boys, or in gallows?

(*The* INSPECTOR *chortles at his little joke.*)

MAN RAY: You want a formal confession? Start writing. I'll dictate.

INSPECTOR: Not so fast, Mr. Ray. Not until I've heard testimony from Rose Sellavie.

MAN RAY: I've told you, that's impossible.

INSPECTOR: Not anymore. I've found her.

DUCHAMP: You've what?

INSPECTOR: Oh, it wasn't easy, gentlemen. She kept herself well camouflaged. An ingenious creation, your Rose. Nevertheless, I've rooted her out. With his eagle eye, Publick here led me straight to her source.

PUBLICK: First time ever my dirty mind paid off.

MAN RAY: It's a trick, Duchamp. He's goading us, hoping we'll slip and say too much.

INSPECTOR: Care to comment, Mr. Doo-Champ?

MAN RAY: Don't say a word.

INSPECTOR: Go ahead. Don't be shy. Tell us her true whereabouts.

(DUCHAMP *is silent.*)

Shall I jog your memory, Mr. Doo-Champ? How about a friendly hint? Constable, give Mr. Doo-Champ the opera gloves.

(PUBLICK *hands* DUCHAMP *the opera gloves from the* INSPECTOR'S *desk.*)

MAN RAY: Oh, shit!

INSPECTOR: Now, if you'd be so kind . . . put them on. We're waiting. All eyes are on you, my friend.

MAN RAY: Don't do it, Duchamp!

INSPECTOR: *Put them on!*

(DUCHAMP *slips on the gloves.*)

Nice. Very nice. How do they fit? The proper size? Now, Constable, give Mr. Doo-Champ the pièce de résistance—the crowning flourish. Pass him the plumes.

(PUBLICK *passes the feathered hat to* DUCHAMP.)

Go ahead. I'm eager to meet the lady. Slap on the feathers and let's see her smile. Marcel Doo-Champ alias Rose Sellavie! Oh, my, my. What a vision. A sight for sore eyes. Look, Publick, we've got a guest. Rose Sellavie, right here in our midst!

(DUCHAMP *takes the hat; he puts it on. He now stands in his well-tailored suit, the opera gloves, and the cascade of feathers. The effect is lodged somewhere between transvestism and the surreal.*

ROSE *appears at the top of the stairs. She is dressed as* DUCHAMP *in a matching men's suit. She also dons opera gloves and her signature hat. In addition, she carries a pipe. Together, she and* DUCHAMP *create mirror images of each other.* DUCHAMP *climbs the stairs to join her, where they strike a tableau.*

The INSPECTOR *is agog.* PUBLICK'S *eyes bulge in disbelief. They watch the following action with varying degrees of wonder and horror. Even* MAN RAY, *accustomed to* DUCHAMP'S *trickery, is astonished.*

The actor who has portrayed ROSE *until this moment in the play will now be referred to as* DUCHAMP II. *Both actors will on occasion assume* ROSE's *liquid identity in their retelling of the mystery.)*

DUCHAMP II: So, Inspector. You think you're clever enough to nip Rose in the bud?

DUCHAMP *(As* ROSE.*)*: *Bonjour*, Man Ray! Still shocking the ladies with your big flashbulb?

MAN RAY *(Blushing.)*: Well hello, Rose!

INSPECTOR: I'll be goddamned . . . Constable, mark every word said. *Now!* I want it all down in writing. Each stutter. Each pause.

*(*PUBLICK *pulls out a pad and pencil and begins scribbling furiously while the twin* DUCHAMPS *spill their story.)*

DUCHAMP *(As* ROSE.*)*: Who can truly be contained by a single sex, Inspector?

DUCHAMP II: Rose was my masterpiece.

(The two DUCHAMPS *descend the stairs, their limbs intertwining in a series of bizarre poses.)*

DUCHAMP *(As* ROSE.*)*: He composed me piece by piece, joint by joint.

DUCHAMP II: Limbs lifted from other notorious nudes.

DUCHAMP *(As* ROSE.*)*: Fragonard's flushed bathers dipping rosy thighs into brine. Boucher's supine Venus. Da Vinci's bulbous Leda and her ornithological Zeus.

*(*DUCHAMP *slithers up to the* CONSTABLE, *who sweats nervously.)*

Ooh-la-la! Such a sweet, baby-faced Constable. Perhaps after the interrogation we could get together for an aperitif, *oui*?

PUBLICK: Aw, Jesus!

(DUCHAMP *distracts him by stroking his hair, meanwhile slipping the gun from his holster.*)

DUCHAMP II: She was born of a thousand paintbrushes and a thousand years. . . .

INSPECTOR: Dress it up any way you like, Doo-Champ. It's still perversion, pure and simple!

(DUCHAMP *fires the gun into the air. There is a sudden, unexpected change in lighting. The stage goes black, except for the large film lights. For the remainder of the confession,* DUCHAMP *and* DUCHAMP II *manipulate the lights, alternately focusing on each other,* MAN RAY, *the* INSPECTOR, *and the* CONSTABLE *to heighten the telling of their tale.*)

DUCHAMP (*As* ROSE.): Nightly in his dreams we would dance!

DUCHAMP II: Remember, *ma chérie,* among my friends, or sitting over chess, how I painted you with words?

DUCHAMP (*As* ROSE.): Often you dropped only my name like a musical note torn from a score. . . .

DUCHAMP II: "My sister Rose composes prose."

DUCHAMP (*As* ROSE.): Or my favorite: "When Rose arose—

DUCHAMP II (*Completing the pun.*): —I rose, aroused!"

(*They laugh, a sound that falls somewhere between infectious and maniacal.*)

DUCHAMP (*As* ROSE.): Soon I began leaving traces of myself about your studio.

DUCHAMP II: You wrote lewd limericks and slipped them beneath my pillow.

DUCHAMP (*As* ROSE.): "A question, *mon cher,* of intimate hygiene, yes? Should one put the hilt of the foil in the quilt of the goil?"

DUCHAMP II: Pornographic puns taped to the mirror . . .

DUCHAMP *(As* ROSE.*):* "An incesticide must sleep with his mother before killing her, *oui?*"

DUCHAMP II: It wasn't long before Man Ray's curiosity was piqued!

*(*DUCHAMP *hurls the spotlight on the* INSPECTOR. DUCHAMP II *aims his spotlight at* MAN RAY.*)*

INSPECTOR: When you first requested to photograph Miss Sellavie, were you aware of her true identity?

MAN RAY: Duchamp said he had a twin sister. Is that so strange?

*(*DUCHAMP *and* DUCHAMP II *quickly turn the lights back on each other.)*

DUCHAMP II: Rose knew how he treated his Bowery models.

DUCHAMP *(As* ROSE.*):* I'll teach him to tangle in my bed of thorns.

DUCHAMP II: I had to give her shape so she might carry out her plan. My own body was the canvas.

DUCHAMP *(As* ROSE.*):* Gloves, gowns, a magnificent hat rimmed with ostrich plumes!

DUCHAMP II: Manners to befit a femme fatale.

DUCHAMP *(As* ROSE.*):* You textured me with erotic appetites and a decadent heart.

DUCHAMP II: A saunter.

DUCHAMP *(As* ROSE.*):* A pout.

DUCHAMP II: Soft eyes.

DUCHAMP *(As* ROSE.*):* And a sneer.

DUCHAMP II: I poured my breath into you and—

DUCHAMP *(As* ROSE.*):* Voilà!

DUCHAMP II: You were complete. I followed my own footsteps out the door and into the darkness.

(DUCHAMP II *keeps his spot aimed at* DUCHAMP, *and* DUCHAMP *shines his at* MAN RAY.)

DUCHAMP (*As* ROSE.): Man Ray, please! Your turn. Don't be coy.

MAN RAY: It was late. I'd been slurping down vodka faster than it would pour. He . . . she . . . Rose showed up at my door.

DUCHAMP II: As I opened my mouth to speak, it was her voice that poured forth, not mine.

DUCHAMP (*As* ROSE.): "It sounds as though you're quite accustomed to strange ladies banging down your door."

MAN RAY: He shut out the lights so I wouldn't see his face. You gotta believe me. I had no idea!

DUCHAMP (*As* ROSE.): He lifted my chin and we kissed!

DUCHAMP II: I felt his whiskers push against mine.

DUCHAMP (*As* ROSE.): Trembling, he peeled off my gloves!

DUCHAMP II: I felt his tongue nibbling on the tips of my fingers.

DUCHAMP (*As* ROSE.): Finally, he heaved my skirt above my head, plucking the garters with his teeth!

PUBLICK: Aw, cripes!

MAN RAY: I've ducked under a thousand skirts, but this was a first! The floor slid clean out from under me! Rose was gone, and there was Duchamp, pinned down on the mattress, his eyes gleaming as if to say—

DUCHAMP (*As himself.*): Aha! I caught you.

DUCHAMP II: As quickly as Rose had consumed me, she disappeared. Man Ray had sought his psyche and found me hiding there.

(DUCHAMP II *swivels his light away from* DUCHAMP *and focuses it on the* INSPECTOR. *Both the* INSPECTOR *and* MAN RAY *are illuminated for the following exchange.*)

INSPECTOR: And still you took pictures. Even after you'd learned the truth.

MAN RAY: I was in a slump! I needed a change.

INSPECTOR: Pity you only had one other sex from which to choose.

MAN RAY: You bet your bottom dollar he posed for me. I made him promise a whole series, right there on the spot! The phantom Rose, torn out of his subconscious and captured on film!

INSPECTOR: Flesh peddlers, both of you.

MAN RAY: You don't understand one whit, do you?

(DUCHAMP II *focuses on* DUCHAMP, *and* DUCHAMP *moves his spot to catch* MAN RAY.)

DUCHAMP *(As* ROSE.*)*: Man Ray flatters himself, Inspector. He pretends to know the whole story when he only knows a fraction.

MAN RAY: There's more?

DUCHAMP *(As* ROSE.*)*: Why, the painting, of course!

DUCHAMP II: Our confession's complete, Rose. It's time to stop.

DUCHAMP *(As* ROSE.*)*: Why, Marcel. It's the best part.

(DUCHAMP *moves his spot from* MAN RAY *to the* INSPECTOR.)

DUCHAMP II: But the Inspector has a pristine mind and a Christian soul. He has no interest in your lecherous tales.

DUCHAMP *(As* ROSE.*)*: No interest in our debauchery? No interest in our final, ruthless night of orgiastic frenzy? None at all?

INSPECTOR: Now hold on a minute, Doo-Champ. I'd like to hear what the little lady's got to say.

DUCHAMP II: Ah, *mon Dieu!* I am crimson with shame, Inspector.

DUCHAMP *(As* ROSE.*)*: Late one night, Marcel came home to find me waiting at the top of the stairs.

(From opposite sides of the stage the DUCHAMPS *focus their lights on the staircase. The beams crisscross, causing shadows to multiply.* DUCHAMP *races to the top of the stairs.* DUCHAMP II *stands at the base. In countless shadows, their figures dance across the rear of the stage.*

The two men shoot their lines back and forth at each other in a tense, staccato rhythm. While the language of the scene is playful, the intensity with which they spar suggests that the stakes of this game are deadly.)

DUCHAMP *(As* ROSE.*)*: Psst! *Mon choux!*

DUCHAMP II: Who is it? Who's there?

DUCHAMP *(As* ROSE.*)*: I'm ready to pose.

DUCHAMP II: No, *ma chérie.* Not tonight.

DUCHAMP *(As* ROSE.*)*: It was "No" yesterday.

DUCHAMP II: And it will be "No" tomorrow.

DUCHAMP *(As* ROSE.*)*: I won't move a muscle. You can capture every inch.

DUCHAMP II: There's no light.

DUCHAMP *(As* ROSE.*)*: We'll burn candles.

DUCHAMP II: There's no paint.

DUCHAMP *(As* ROSE.*)*: Your box is full.

DUCHAMP II: My palette knife is dull.

DUCHAMP *(As* ROSE.*)*: Newly sharpened.

DUCHAMP II: You devil, Rose. You'd let me hang by a noose to hang by a nail.

DUCHAMP *(As* ROSE.*)*: You've let me live inside your head, you've let me walk the streets, and still you won't commit me to canvas.

DUCHAMP II: You've been photographed? Isn't that enough?

DUCHAMP (*As* ROSE.): I'm lodged in your brain, and a few camera flashes won't burn me away.

DUCHAMP II: Let Man Ray execute you. He's a better shot.

DUCHAMP (*As* ROSE.): Don't you have the courage to execute your own creations?

DUCHAMP II: You're a hollow pose. An erotic fancy. *Eros, c'est la vie!* Your whole life is built on nothing more than a pun.

DUCHAMP (*As* ROSE.): So what's the risk? Start sketching.

DUCHAMP II: I'm sorry, *ma chérie*, but you're not worth the paint.

DUCHAMP (*As* ROSE.): Then model for me.

DUCHAMP II: What?

DUCHAMP (*As* ROSE.): Go ahead. Slip into my skin.

DUCHAMP II: Don't be foolish. What for?

DUCHAMP (*As* ROSE.): You won't paint my picture, so what can I do? Paint my own, yes? A self-portrait. You'll be my mirror.

DUCHAMP II: You'll trap me into painting your portrait, eh, Rose?

DUCHAMP (*As* ROSE.): *Oui*, Marcel. Frame you into framing me.

DUCHAMP II: Duping oneself can be dangerous.

DUCHAMP (*As* ROSE.): You were never one to refuse a good game.

DUCHAMP II: Ah, *mon Dieu!* If my reputation's at peril, I accept!

DUCHAMP (*As* ROSE.): So pass me your pipe.

(DUCHAMP II *passes his pipe to* DUCHAMP. DUCHAMP *puffs on it, dropping* ROSE'*s demeanor.*

DUCHAMP II *now adopts the role of* ROSE.)

DUCHAMP II (*As* ROSE.): "A Rose pose, *oui*? A femme fatale? A camp vamp? Pass me on the street and your prick'll prickle! *Ooh-la-la!*"

DUCHAMP:

> "A RECIPE FOR ROSE
> by M. Duchamp
> Wrench her thighs from Rubens
> And her bottom from Boucher
> Deck her crotch in Delacroix
> And her mind in Yves Tanguy!"

DUCHAMP II (As ROSE.): "C'est magnifique! Bravo, Marcel! Bravo!"

DUCHAMP: "Mesdames and Messieurs, for my next feat—a poem in paint! Rose deflowered! Petal by petal and piece by piece!"

DUCHAMP II (As ROSE.): "No! Boo! Hiss!"

DUCHAMP: "Quiet in the gallery!"

DUCHAMP II (As ROSE.): "But we've seen it before! Every carnival huckster! Every medicine show! The magician! The coffin! The lady! The saw!"

DUCHAMP: "But in my trick we don't put back the pieces!"

(Darkly.)

The game is over, Rose.

(DUCHAMP II drops the role of ROSE immediately. Now the two men are virtually indistinguishable. They stalk each other, up and down the stairs.)

DUCHAMP II: What's this? You can't change the rules midstream.

DUCHAMP: Life from a new angle, yes?

DUCHAMP II: But I created you. I'm flesh and blood. You're just an idea!

DUCHAMP: The shoes have been switched.

DUCHAMP II: No. This is absurd.

DUCHAMP: The table's turned.

DUCHAMP II: Don't come any closer.

DUCHAMP: Your mind's in a somersault, *ma chérie*!

DUCHAMP II: I never wanted to pose for you!

DUCHAMP: Your shadow has stolen your soul, yes?

DUCHAMP II: You're mad! Your eyes are both prisms! Your head's jammed with puzzles!

DUCHAMP: And it is scrambling the pieces . . .

DUCHAMP II: Loopy Leonardo! Raving Rembrandt!

DUCHAMP: I joined your limbs together; I can unjoin them, too!

DUCHAMP II: You'll make my breasts obelisks and my bottom cubes!

(DUCHAMP *pulls a palette knife from his pocket and raises it in the air. It glistens. Simultaneously,* DUCHAMP II *withdraws his palette knife. They circle each other dangerously.*)

DUCHAMP: Get away from me!

DUCHAMP II: You think I'm weak, don't you? I'm much stronger than you! I've weathered the ancients, and I'll weather the moderns, too!

DUCHAMP: Go ahead!

DUCHAMP II: Cut into me!

DUCHAMP: We'll bleed together!

DUCHAMP II: A final portrait—Rose!

(*Each raises his knife, ready to strike.*)

Lights play across the large upstage canvas. With a loud creak, accompanied by the deafening sound of machinery, the canvas collapses. The two DUCHAMPS *disappear and an enormous rendering of Duchamp's painting* Nude Descending a Staircase *is revealed. The staircase itself seems to jut forth from the painting's composition. The image of the fragmented nude consumes the stage.*

Blackout. In the darkness, an eerie, almost muted voice whistles the song heard earlier, "La Vie en Rose."

Lights slowly rise on the precinct office. The INSPECTOR *has all but collapsed at his desk.* PUBLICK *stands with his mouth open.* MAN RAY *breaks into slow, loud applause.* DUCHAMP II *stands at the base of the huge painting, smiling ever so slightly. He has removed the gloves and the hat, and now stands dressed in his customary suit. The original* DUCHAMP *is nowhere to be seen.)*

INSPECTOR *(Slowly, then gaining momentum.)*: Riddle me this, Mr. Artiste. Mr. Painter. Why didn't you stay at home today and read the paper over coffee, or have a nice midmorning nap? Why didn't you go for a stroll in the park? Why didn't you throw yourself under a fucking train? Why the hell did you walk in here and destroy my day? This morning I knew right from left, but this afternoon I can't be sure! Men turning into women and back again at the drop of a hat! Arms and legs akimbo in the air! I don't like it! It's not the way the world should be!

DUCHAMP II *(Gently.)*: Then perhaps you can paint a different picture for us, yes?

INSPECTOR: Get out. Get the hell away from here. I don't want the two of you crowding decent prisons, rabble-rousing and spreading ideas. Constable, throw them out.

DUCHAMP II: Inspector, please. You should sit down, put your feet up, have a smoke.

*(*DUCHAMP II *gently steers the* INSPECTOR *into his chair.)*

Thank you so much for your hospitality.

(PUBLICK *gestures toward the scale rendition of the painting that he con-fiscated earlier from* DUCHAMP*'s apartment.*)

PUBLICK: What should we do with the evidence, Chief?

INSPECTOR: Fuel for the boiler room!

DUCHAMP: Let me keep it, Inspector.

INSPECTOR: Go ahead, Doo-Champ. Keep hacking yourself up and calling the pieces art. Where will it get you? You'll be a laughing stock.

MAN RAY: Spoken like a seasoned critic, Inspector!

PUBLICK: And the skintypes, Chief?

(MAN RAY *makes a quick grab for the birdcage.*)

INSPECTOR: I've no use for them, Mr. Ray. I shudder to think of their value to you.

(MAN RAY *reaches into the birdcage and pulls out a single photograph of* ROSE, *which he offers to* PUBLICK.)

MAN RAY: Souvenir?

(PUBLICK *hesitates, then grabs the photo and stuffs it in his jacket.* MAN RAY *smiles.*)

Sometime I'd like to take a picture of what lurks in your head. Constable. I bet we could blow the roof off this joint.

INSPECTOR: Out, I said! Out, out, out!

DUCHAMP: *Au revoir*, Inspector. Constable. May your days be filled with more manageable crimes!

(DUCHAMP *picks up his painting and heads for the door.* MAN RAY *follows with the birdcage. On his way out,* DUCHAMP *gestures toward the coat rack standing idly by the exit. Under his breath, he whispers to* MAN RAY.)

Psst! Coat rack!

(Slyly, MAN RAY *scoops up the coat rack. The two men slip out the door and into darkness.)*

INSPECTOR: Lock the door. Bolt the window. I don't want them coming back.

*(*PUBLICK *follows orders.)*

PUBLICK: Helluva day, Chief.

INSPECTOR: What say we keep today's adventures to ourselves.

PUBLICK: You kidding? Who'd believe it?

INSPECTOR: We'll file no report. We'll keep mum before the Commissioner. Agreed?

PUBLICK: Me. I been playing cards all day. I ain't heard a peep, or seen nothing.

INSPECTOR: Thatta boy, Publick.

PUBLICK: Just another routine day.

INSPECTOR: Ordinary. Uneventful.

PUBLICK: Downright dull.

(Both men attempt to sit calmly. Instead, they form a cacophony of fidgets and ticks. A long pause. Finally, the silence becomes unbearable. PUBLICK *clears his throat and wipes the sweat off his brow.)*

Yo, Chief. Don't say I told you, but there's whiskey hidden in the lockup. You could use a glass. We could both use a glass. Back in a jiff.

*(*PUBLICK *exits. The* INSPECTOR *sighs.)*

INSPECTOR: My screws must be loose. I must be losing my mind. I got my own nightmares. I don't need his.

(He shakes his head for a moment, sighs again, then shudders in an imaginary breeze. After shaking off the chill, he opens the day's newspaper.

The door of the precinct office opens. ROSE SELAVY—*this time portrayed by* DUCHAMP—*enters, in full regalia. The gloves. The hat. The magnificent wrap. She pauses to speak.)*

ROSE SELAVY: Pardon, monsieur.

(The INSPECTOR *lowers his paper.* ROSE *smiles.)*

I wish to report a crime . . .

(The INSPECTOR *stares, transfixed.)*

Watbanaland

Watbanaland was originally produced by the WPA Theater (Kyle Renick, artistic director; Lori Sherman, managing director) in New York City on March 18, 1995. It was directed by Christopher Ashley; the set design was by Rob Odorisio; the costume design was by Anne C. Patterson; the lighting design was by Donald Holder; the music and sound design were by Guy Sherman/Aural Fixation; and the production stage manager was Kate Broderick. The cast was as follows:

FLO . . . . Lisa Emery

MARILYN . . . . Emily Skinner

PARK . . . . David Chandler

DASH . . . . Ken Garito

PENELOPE WAX . . . . Susan Greenhill

YOBO MUNDE . . . . Dion Graham

CHARACTERS

FLO
> A well-coiffed woman in her late thirties.

MARILYN
> A tough cookie from one of the outer boroughs.

PARK
> Forty; of the blue blood, Brooks Brothers variety.

DASH
> A toll-booth attendant with perfect DNA.

PENELOPE WAX
> A vivacious television personality.

YOBO MUNDE
> A third world father, articulate and with great dignity.

SETTING

New York City, Watbanaland, and Springfield.

ACT ONE

Scene 1

FLO *sits high on a stool, holding a picture book. She wears pearls and a bright-colored gingham apron with an apple appliqué. In a pleasant, well-modulated voice she reads to a room full of children.*

FLO: "Mr. Hodge-Podge was a curious fellow, with green suspenders and eyes like cupcakes." Ruthie, be quiet. It's my turn to talk now.

(FLO raises the book higher.)

Better? We can all see if we keep our heads down. "Every morning, he set out with his junk cart, collecting collectibles from rubbish bins and back stoops." Ruthie, stay on your own blanket. That blanket belongs to Melanie. "All day long Mr. Hodge-Podge tinkered, making marvelous inventions from broken baubles and throwaway toys. One fine spring day, Mr. Hodge-Podge made a miracle. With two old shoes and a wastebasket, with old bubble gum and a bicycle tire, Mr. Hodge-Podge built a little boy."

(FLO pauses for a moment, regarding what she has just read with a critical eye. She continues.)

"He had ball bearings for eyes, and soup spoons instead of proper ears."

(FLO stops reading. She stares at the book, aghast.)

This book is a *fiction*, boys and girls. This book is a *lie*. Contrary to what this author would have you believe, children are not fashioned from refuse. They are not salvaged from leftovers or pieced together from broken parts.

(FLO *begins tearing out the book's pages in a slow, methodical manner.*)

When a man loves a woman, he inserts his penis into her vagina. This is known as sexual intercourse. The male reproductive cell, the sperm, penetrates the female reproductive cell, the ovum, and with Nature's blessing fetal growth occurs. That, children, is how babies get born. Bad book. Bad, bad book. We'll burn the pages of this book in the paint sink.

(FLO *pulls a lighter from her apron pocket. She ignites the pages and lets them burn, one by one, dropping them into a rainbow-splattered sink.*)

Stop crying, Ruthie. Stop crying before Mrs. Stillman gives you something to cry about.

(FLO *drops the remainder of the book into the sink. Flames blaze upward, illuminating her face from beneath.*)

Stand back, class. Shh. Farther, farther. Damn it, Ruthie! You'll singe your pinafore. Cotton is flammable, and so are little girls. That's the way. Quiet now. Nobody move.

(Blackout.)

Scene 2

MARILYN *sits behind a desk, flipping the pages of a fashion magazine in rhythm to heavy-metal music blaring from a transistor radio.* MARILYN *has a mountainous yellow mane of curls. She wears pointed pink heels with baby-blue toe guards. She taps them against the thick plastic carpet shield that underlies her desk.*

The telephone rings. MARILYN *stares at it. It rings again. She picks up.*

MARILYN: Mr. Stillman's office . . . Speak up . . . Louder . . . Oh. Hello, Mrs. Stillman . . . This afternoon, like today? . . . I'll tell him . . . I'll remind him . . . I can't make him, can I . . . I don't have a leash. . . . Thank you for calling, Mrs. Stillman.

(MARILYN *plops down the phone.* PARK *enters. He carries a loose memo.* PARK *places the memo on the desktop over* MARILYN'S *magazine. He clicks off her radio.*)

PARK: Did you type this memorandum?

MARILYN: So?

PARK: Who is Mr. Snoth? Who is Mr. Snoth, and why am I selling munificent bonds?

MARILYN: I give up.

PARK: I'm not accusing, Marilyn; I'm only quizzical.

MARILYN: So ask me something I know.

PARK: Who is Mr. Smith?

MARILYN: Your squash partner, every Thursday.

PARK: What are municipal bonds?

(MARILYN *sighs heavily, glares at* PARK, *and crumples the memo into a tight little ball.*)

MARILYN: Your handwriting's for shit.

(MARILYN *gets up from her desk and slings her purse over her shoulder.*)

I'm going to lunch.

PARK: Now? This minute?

MARILYN: No. This minute, I am going to the ladies' room. I got a Portuguese man-o'-war living in my gut. Then I'm going to lunch.

PARK: This memo is a catalog of errors. Munificent bonds. Government tissues. Mock exchange!

MARILYN: I'm not trimming my nails. Took two years to grow these.

PARK: Sit down at your computer. Blow the dust off the keys. I'd like a letter-perfect draft on my desk in five minutes.

MARILYN: I got a date.

PARK: Five minutes, Marilyn!

MARILYN: I told you, I got a date.

PARK: With what?

MARILYN: My date is a who. I do not date "whats."

PARK: With *whom* are you dining today, Marilyn?

MARILYN: With Dash.

PARK: Dash is a toll-booth attendant.

MARILYN: Dash is none of your business.

PARK: My Business is my business! My Business is your business, too, and your business at my Business is this goddamn memorandum!

MARILYN: Whatsa matter? You got something against Dash?

PARK: Please, Marilyn.

MARILYN: You got something against the common man?

PARK: Sit. Type.

MARILYN: Mr. Park Avenue. Mr. Mercedes-Benz.

PARK: For form's sake. Please.

MARILYN: Dash is double-muscled. You don't get that working out; it's in the genes. Dash has a very high IQ.

PARK: Please!

MARILYN: Dash has *real good chromosomes*. Scientists at major universities have performed *tests*. His DNA was featured in a *major medical magazine*. Top-notch.

PARK: That's enough.

MARILYN: You ever had your cells put under a microscope? You ever had that kind of courage?

PARK: Go to lunch, Marilyn.

MARILYN: 'Cause I have.

PARK: Go to lunch!

(Pause.)

MARILYN: Saturday is Milo's first birthday. That's something, huh? His little heart beating three hundred and sixty-five days.

(Pause.)

Dash wants to buy him a present. He's been saving up. Ten dollars every month. Dash is gonna let me choose.

(Another pause. PARK stares at MARILYN. He pulls his wallet from his jacket pocket, licks his thumb and forefinger, and pulls out a one-hundred-dollar bill. He places it on the desk before MARILYN.)

F.A.O. Schwarz, they got this stuffed lion in the window. I don't know which is bigger—the toy or the price tag.

(PARK removes another bill and places it on top of the first.)

PARK: Buy him something colorful. Something he can stroke.

(MARILYN folds the bills and puts them in her purse. She starts to leave.)

MARILYN: Thanks . . . boss.

PARK: Marilyn?

MARILYN: Huh, what?

PARK: Perhaps it's time to rethink our arrangement.

MARILYN: How so?

PARK: Your employment.

MARILYN: You threatening me?

PARK: I've stuck my neck out as far as it will go. You can't type. Lotus, dBase, perish the thought! Still, you're the highest paid executive assistant at the firm.

MARILYN: I got expenses.

PARK: Not to mention the *perks*. The Christmas bonus. The Easter bonus. The Arbor Day bonus.

MARILYN: Every month, big expenses.

PARK: It's only natural that people should wonder. That people should *posit theories*.

MARILYN: Only one way to stop gossip I know of.

PARK: Yes, and what's that?

MARILYN: Tell the truth.

PARK: Don't mock me.

MARILYN: I could put it in a memo.

PARK: Miss Klepowski . . .

MARILYN: It is not my fault you hired me with no secretarial skills. It is not my fault your wife once took a long weekend in Ticonderoga. It is not my fault that I was frightened and you seized opportunity and that I turned out to be Catholic.

PARK: Lower your voice. *Please.*

MARILYN: You cut us loose . . . you are gonna be front page on the company newsletter, Mr. Stillman.

PARK *(Barely a croak.)*: I am sorry.

MARILYN: Huh, what?

PARK: I am sorry.

MARILYN: You sure are.

PARK: Have . . . have a good lunch.

*(*MARILYN *smiles. She turns to go.)*

MARILYN: Christ, I almost forgot. Your wife called. Said you gotta go to the doctor today. Or else. She said I should make you go.

Said I should force you. I asked her, "How? I don't got a *leash*, lady."

(PARK *stands, forlorn.*)

Back in a few.

(MARILYN *exits.* PARK *stands, swaying almost imperceptibly. He plucks the memo off the desk. He uncrumples it. He tears into it savagely with his teeth. Pause. Slowly, contemplatively,* PARK *begins to chew. Blackout.*)

Scene 3

PARK *and* FLO *sit side by side at a handsomely waxed wooden table. On the table is a sleek black tape recorder.*

In front of them sits an invisible doctor.

PARK: What is this?

FLO: Shh, honey.

PARK: Don't people write anymore? Don't people take notes?

FLO: Relax, Park.

PARK: Where do you store the tapes?

FLO: Really.

PARK: Are they secure? Are they kept confidential, under lock and key?

FLO: She broadcasts them every Sunday morning over the radio.

PARK: Can we keep the tapes?

FLO: Park . . .

PARK: I'd like to keep the tapes.

FLO: What for?

PARK: In a safe-deposit box.

FLO: Why don't you swallow them, whole, like a stolen key?

PARK: What I do with them doesn't matter. What matters is confiscation.

(Pause. PARK and FLO lock eyes for a moment.)

FLO: Park would like you to know, Doctor, that he is not here of his
own volition. I made our appointment. I drove the car. I put
coinage in the meter.

PARK: Flo.

FLO: I pressed the appropriate floor.

PARK: I am here, aren't I? I am here today, this instant, right now. I
am not coming here again. Understood?

(Pause. FLO abruptly turns to face the doctor, breaking the silence.)

FLO: At first we were diligent. At first we were persistent. Now our
efforts have waned.

PARK: Not entirely.

FLO: Now, Park . . .

PARK: Tell her, Flo. Our efforts have not altogether ceased.

(FLO is silent.)

     Tell her.

FLO: I won't lie, Park.

(Pause.)

PARK: I see no reason, Doctor . . . I see no reason to subject ourselves . . . our marriage . . . to routine disappointment. Not
while the cause is a mystery. An unknown. I fail, Doctor, to understand our failure.

(Pause.)

FLO: Thirteen months.

PARK: Flo . . .

FLO: It has been thirteen months, two weeks, and four days.

PARK: I can't will it to happen, Doctor. I can't flip a switch. It is not a dog, panting and wagging to please. Sit up, sit down, roll over. It doesn't respond to commands.

FLO: It doesn't respond at all.

(Pause.)

PARK: The standard posture, tried and true.

FLO: I have done my best to encourage variations, Doctor, but my suggestions are routinely met with disdain, even . . . disgust.

PARK: The *Kama Sutra* is a fiction. The normal body, however fit, is incapable of inverting itself so completely. Permuting itself beyond recognition. It is foolish and inhibiting to shelve such books on our night table. The doctor, I'm certain, will concur. Yes?

(Pause.)

No, I'm sorry. I can't envision myself standing before some smarmy adolescent inquiring if *Lust Busters* is available for rental. Furthermore, Doctor, I have seen enough to know such films are anti-erotic. They are, in fact, medical. I would sooner watch brain surgery. Shock therapy. Castration.

(Pause.)

Toys? Bobbing about on the bed with rubber parts? Candy underclothes? Acting like babies in hopes of yielding one? Don't insult us, Doctor.

(Pause.)

Don't sit smugly and prescribe. We are not automatons. We are not broken clocks.

FLO: Park—

PARK: You don't know us. You don't know me.

(*A long pause.* PARK *fumes.* FLO *shifts ever so slightly in her seat.*)

FLO (*Finally, in a small voice.*): Do you want a child, Park?

PARK: I'm here. I'm trying.

FLO: Do you want my child?

PARK: What?

(FLO *turns away.*)

I'm doing the best I can.

(*Pause.* FLO *looks imploringly at* PARK.)

Don't look at me. Don't stare. It doesn't help the situation. It doesn't exactly move things along.

FLO: I wish it were a tumor.

PARK: Don't.

FLO: I wish it were poison running through my body like blood. Then they could transfuse.

PARK: That's enough.

FLO: It's me, isn't it? It's what I am to you.

(FLO *places her hand over her face. She begins to cry.*)

PARK: I want. I want so very much. If you could see inside my head. If you could know. Doctor. Help us. Help me. I'll try. I am trying, Flo.

FLO: Park?

PARK: Yes?

FLO: I love you?

(PARK *doesn't respond.*)

Yes?

PARK *(Quietly.)*: Help.

(PARK and FLO don't move. Blackout.)

Scene 4

A pretzel stand. MARILYN *is drinking a soda. She dabs her lips with a napkin from a metal dispenser.*

Standing beside her, bursting out of its wrapping, is a huge stuffed lion.

DASH *is standing on the opposite side of the lion. He has a jumbo pretzel, loaded with mustard, in front of him. He has dark wavy hair and a powerful frame. Several gold chains and a bulky wristwatch brighten his otherwise drab uniform.*

MARILYN: Dash?

DASH: Yo.

MARILYN: You ever get tired, working the tolls?

DASH: Nah. I love it. It's like being stuck upright in a casket. Big glass coffin in the middle of the fucking road.

(Pause.)

MARILYN: Dash?

DASH: Yo.

MARILYN: Bite?

(DASH pushes the pretzel in MARILYN's direction. MARILYN picks it up and takes a bite.)

DASH: Whoa. You bit the fucking thing in two. Goddamn alligator.

MARILYN: One little bite!

DASH: That is not a bite. That is a meal. You took a goddamn banquet.

MARILYN: I'm hungry.

DASH: So get your own.

MARILYN: I don't want a *whole* one.

(*Pause. They chew.*)

DASH: So how come you got two hundred dollars?

MARILYN: You put too much mustard on your goddamn pretzel.

DASH: I save up a hundred bucks for the kid. That's a three-hundred-dollar lion. He's gonna get an attitude.

MARILYN: Milo's not gonna get an attitude.

DASH: You start him on three-hundred-dollar lions, he's gonna get a very definite attitude. A very King of the Jungle attitude. You ever seen a kid with that advanced degree of attitude?

MARILYN: Maybe.

DASH: You let me come round.

MARILYN: You don't wanna come round.

DASH: Let me. I'll fix this kid.

MARILYN: He's too young to play. He lies there. He wets. You're not missing any miracles.

DASH: Too young to play, and you got him a three-hundred-dollar doll?

MARILYN: He can look at it.

DASH: You got two hundred extra greenbacks and you want this kid looking at stuff? Hell, get him wide-screen TV. Get him hockey tickets, you want him to look.

MARILYN: It's his birthday.

DASH: Mr. Stillman give you that money?

MARILYN: I gotta get back to the office.

DASH: The rent, too? He pick up that? The panty hose you're wearing? Your cheese Danish in the morning and your Chianti at
night?

(He squeezes her behind.)

He pay for your tattoo?

MARILYN: Fuck you.

DASH: You ever written a check, babe? In your own hand?

(MARILYN grabs her purse and scoops up the pretzel.)

Put down the pretzel! That is not your pretzel!

MARILYN: You gotta get back to the tunnel.

DASH: Put down the goddamn cracker!

MARILYN: You don't go back, who's taking your booth? Could be
empty this minute. Cars could be shooting through your booth
without a cent. Who's gonna collect the nickels and dimes, eh,
Dash?

(DASH swipes the pretzel from MARILYN.)

DASH: If your boss gave you two hundred dollars, you keep it quiet.
For your own safety. I don't wanna know.

(Savagely, DASH bites into the pretzel. He finishes it. He gulps.)

So did he?

MARILYN: You smell like asphalt.

DASH: I saved up ten months. Ten months for a kid I got no proof
exists.

MARILYN: That makes me happy, that you did that.

DASH: I'm not splitting that gift with some dick. Some limp-dick
Rockefeller.

MARILYN: Good. Fine.

DASH: I'm not splitting anything with him. Got that?

MARILYN: Yeah.

DASH: Come here.

MARILYN: I hafta go.

(DASH pulls MARILYN to him.)

DASH: Kiss me.

MARILYN: I got mustard all over my tongue.

DASH: Me, too. Let's make a tongue sandwich.

MARILYN: Gross!

(He pulls her face against his, and they kiss for a long time.)

You wanna see my kid?

DASH: Hell, yes. Let me meet this Milo kid.

MARILYN: I dint say you could *meet* him. I said you could *see* him.

(DASH kneels.)

DASH: With all my heart, with all my skin, with all my guts, and my bones, I wanna see this kid.

MARILYN: You come pick me up after work, O.K.?

DASH: We go to your mother's, I gotta get me a tie.

MARILYN: We're not going to my mother's.

DASH: You told me he lives with your mother.

MARILYN: He don't.

DASH: I never seen his crib at your place. I never seen his toys.

MARILYN: Milo don't live with me.

DASH: What, he got his own place? One year old, he got a condo, a bachelor pad, what?

MARILYN: Just pick me up, O.K.? In the lobby.

DASH: I'll come up.

MARILYN: At the elevators downstairs.

DASH: Mr. Stillman don't like me coming up? He don't like my ass on his furniture? He don't like I put my grubby fingers on his *Forbes* magazines?

MARILYN: Not so loud.

DASH: He don't like our germs meeting and fucking on little puffs of air?

MARILYN: It's been two hours. I gotta get the phones.

DASH: You let him see your kid?

MARILYN: I gotta go!

DASH: Answer me.

MARILYN: No. He never ast.

DASH: Marilyn?

MARILYN: Tonight, Dash. I gotta go.

(DASH *grabs* MARILYN's *arm.*)

Huh, what?

(DASH *pulls* MARILYN *to him a second time.*)

DASH: Fix me another sandwich.

(*He pulls her face to his, and they kiss again. Even longer this time. Blackout.*)

Scene 5

The bedroom of the Stillmans' apartment.

PARK, *in glasses, sits in an easy chair, reading a book.*

FLO *is at her vanity table, staring into the mirror.*

FLO: I have a pupil. Ruthie. She has the smell of talcum, and her skin boasts a rosiness I've seen in nineteenth-century portraiture more often than in life. Playing near the swing set, when the sun strikes her, she surpasses Cassatt. Today I watched her play for the better part of an hour. She took a doll from its wooden bed. She sat with it till the morning's end, rocking and singing softly. Her fluid eyes stared with wonder into its painted ones. When it was time to nap, she cradled it next to her breast as she slept. Her mother came to retrieve her at the end of the day. Ruthie saw her and broke into unabashed squeals. Her mother laughed too, and knelt down. Ruthie ran to her. They folded into each other. Her mother stood, Ruthie's legs wrapped about her torso. The child seemed to extend, full-blown, from her mother's belly. Ruthie still held the doll, like a torch. Its arms twisted in exultation and its head faced backward. It sprouted forth, like an extra limb, from Ruthie's grasp. The children, real and imagined, were glorious branches, splitting off and reaching toward the sky, taking flight from their parent tree. I watched the three of them and I wished with all my heart for an ax to chop them down.

(FLO *shifts her gaze, regarding* PARK *in the mirror.*)

Deliver me. Deliver me from that.

(PARK *closes his book. He stares at* FLO*'s image in the mirror.*)

PARK: Flo?

FLO: Please?

PARK (*Sternly.*): Enough.

(*Blackout.*)

Scene 6

In the darkness, the disembodied voice of a television set.

THE TELEVISION: Tune in tomorrow at midnight for four hours of nonstop comedy: Jerry Frayne stars in *Oh No, More Pigs!* and Regina Bowles causes trouble aplenty in *The Romp*. Now stay tuned for paid programming.

(The blue flicker of the set reveals a large double bed. PARK *lies in a fetal position, with the pillow over his head.* FLO *is sitting upright, staring at the screen. On the television,* PENELOPE WAX. *She is glamorous, with designer safari gear.)*

PENELOPE WAX: Good evening. My name is Penelope Wax. Many of you already know me as the free-spirited Vera Dent in the hit series *LoveQuest 99*. Off-camera, I play a very different role: national spokesperson for the Famine Fund. Don't flip your dial. Don't turn away. The story I'm going to share with you tonight doesn't have a laugh track. It wasn't filmed before a live studio audience. Still, it could change your life forever.

(The sound of cow bells and the cries of children rise in the distance.)

Here in Watbanaland, death is as constant as the sun's pitiless gaze. Meet Baku. Although he weighs barely twenty pounds, Baku is a proud five years old. Hunger has waged war on Baku's body, a battle that Baku is rapidly losing. A lack of healthy grains means a lack of vitamin A and almost certain blindness. Impure drinking water carries with it a variety of deadly parasites. Too weak to walk or even bat the flies from his brow, Baku lies still on the straw floor of his father's lean-to.

(FLO crawls to the edge of the bed. Her face is reflected in the television's glow.)

But we can help. There are millions of children like Baku, all across the veld region. They are crying out for your spare change. For the cost of a magazine, you could feed Baku for a month. For the cost of a movie, your dollars can provide the medical care this child so desperately needs.

(PENELOPE WAX *steps out of the television and enters the bedroom.* FLO *is stunned.)*

Adopt Baku.

(PENELOPE *takes* FLO*'s hand, gently.)*

You can't bring him into your home, but you can bring him into your heart. For scant pennies a day, you can know the fullness that comes with giving life. Giving a future. Together with the Famine Fund, you can nurture God's greatest gift to the world: a growing child.

(FLO *stares at* PENELOPE WAX, *transfixed.* PARK *does not move. Blackout.)*

Scene 7

Moonlight streams through an open window. It illuminates rumpled bedding: DASH *and* MARILYN *are making love.*

Something's wrong. DASH *stops. He pulls away and sits on the edge of the bed.* MARILYN*'s befuddled.*

MARILYN: Yoo-hoo. Earth to Dash.

(Pause.)

DASH: That kid you got is a real sweet kid.

(Violently, MARILYN *grabs the sheets and wraps them around herself.)*

MARILYN: Screw you.

DASH: You think I would joke? Jesus, Marilyn! You think I got a heart like a tin can?

MARILYN: Don't do this. You don't hafta.

DASH: I'd buy that kid a jungle. If he ast, I'd buy it.

MARILYN: He bothers you, doesn't he?

DASH: Cheetahs and shit. Zebras. I'd buy it.

MARILYN: He bothers you a lot.

DASH: It's a shock, babe. That's all.

(Pause.)

MARILYN: I know what you're thinking. "I can't stay with her. No way. I got super-duper sperm, and she's got rotten eggs."

DASH: Whoa, Mare. Slow down.

MARILYN: *Well, I ain't to blame.* I been to the doctor. He shot me full a dye. I saw my own uterus on a television screen. And it was beautiful. Like a constellation.

DASH: Marilyn. MARE-O-LYNN. That kid you got? You know what he is? He's a surprise bonus.

MARILYN: Dash.

DASH: Yo.

MARILYN: Nothing. You're sweet, that's all. You're a good person.

(Pause.)

DASH: So . . . ah . . . who?

MARILYN: Aw, Christ. Don't start.

DASH: Who left you with that?

MARILYN: Dash, that is not fair. You agreed.

DASH: Tell me.

MARILYN: You have seen Milo. Isn't that enough? I feel that kid on my back every second of every goddamn day. I have to apologize for every breath that boy takes. I gotta answer to you now, too?

DASH: I gotta know.

MARILYN: You wanna stay with me now? Go to sleep. You wanna talk, tell it to the fucking moon.

(Pause.)

DASH: Quit your job.

MARILYN: You crazy?

DASH: You're not working for that man.

MARILYN: I work for whoever I want.

DASH: He's bought you out, baby, and you don't even know it.

MARILYN: I got insurance in my job, Dash! That kid does not run on apple sauce!

DASH: What the hell do you think he's paying you for?

MARILYN: For Milo!

DASH: So he can sleep at night. He don't give two shits about your baby.

(Pause.)

MARILYN: So what am I gonna do? Huh?

DASH: Pull Milo outta that place. All those fat busybodies in white caps, smelling like hand cream and piss. That's a place for old people, not a place for kids.

MARILYN: He needs doctors.

DASH: They ain't doctors, they're mad scientists. They don't keep kids there, they keep experiments.

MARILYN: What about his machines, eh? I can't just *unplug* him. *He ain't a lamp. My kid ain't no toaster.*

DASH: Crammed in a glass box all day. Just like yours truly.

MARILYN: He's *hermetically sealed*.

DASH: What, like a canned ham?

MARILYN: He's *incubated*.

DASH: We'll take him someplace big. Someplace open.

MARILYN: Where? Your place in Corona? My mother in Ozone Park?

DASH: You ever looked at a map? You know that green patch between New York and Disneyland?

MARILYN: Huh, what?

DASH: The breadbasket. *The fruited plain*. We'll go there.

MARILYN: Who are you, deciding these things for me? This is my life, Dash.

DASH: That kid pierced right through me. I looked at him lying there—that protective bonnet, all those needles, trussed up like a Thanksgiving turkey—and fuck. I thought about my world-famous ribosomes, my golden nuclei, my fucking fantabulous deoxyribonucleic acids, and for the first time in my life I felt ashamed. If I were a photograph, that kid, he'd be my negative. Two sides of the same picture. A man's gotta look out for those less fortunate than himself.

MARILYN: So talk particulars.

DASH: I'll quit working the booths. Work my way up to highway patrol. Those cops make good money.

MARILYN: How much?

DASH: Whatever he's paying you, I'll bring home.

MARILYN: I got a difficult life, Dash, but I got it balanced.

DASH: You got one trump card, baby, and right now he's hooked up to jumper cables. Face facts, little miss. Lose the kid, and what happens? You lose your job. Your apartment. Your handouts. What then? You lie back, wait for a guy on a white horse? Well, he's here—saddled up and ready to ride. You wanna end up living life all alone?

MARILYN: No.

DASH: Most guys, they won't take the package. They may dig you, but they'll draw the line. Me, I'll take the package. You'd be a fucking idiot to turn me down.

MARILYN: Is this sweet talk? You mashing me? Don Juan.

DASH: You like us?

MARILYN: Yeah. Maybe.

DASH: Do you love us?

MARILYN: Who knows? Dash, I'm not asking you to be some hero.

DASH: Hey, Marilyn.

MARILYN: Huh, what?

DASH: You forgot. Look at me. You forgot.

MARILYN: Forgot what?

DASH: My DNA. I got superhuman genes.

(MARILYN *considers this for a moment. Blackout.*)

Scene 8

The nurses' station at a large metropolitan hospital. Night. PARK *makes inquiries to an invisible nurse.*

PARK: Klepowski, comma Milo. Perhaps it is cross-referenced. "Baby X." It's a thick file for such a small child.

No, I do not wish to see *him*. I would, however, like to see *his physician*. About the feeding tube. Procedures for its . . . removal.

Solo, please. *Con no madre*. I foot the bill, not she. You'll note in his record that *my* insurance policy covers the protein packs. The catheters. Your salary.

Her consent? Yes. Well. *Este es el problema, no es?* She'll withhold it, I know. She'll fight every inch of the—

The baby is her dividend. The baby is an account at Bergdorf's. A time-share in Bermuda. Please.

(He reads the nurse's name tag.)

"H. Martinez."

(A personal appeal.)

Ms. Martinez. Milo is a hungry baby, and he is eating me alive.

(Blackout.)

Scene 9

The living room of the Stillmans' apartment.

PARK *sits at a small desk, with an open ledger.* FLO *needlepoints.*

PARK: How odd.

FLO: Hmm?

PARK: These checks. There's no mention of these checks on the ledger.

FLO: I've been remiss.

PARK: When you write a check, make a note.

FLO: I apologize.

PARK: In the future—

FLO: Yes. In the future, I'll note each check. I'll deduct each total from the remaining balance listed on the pink line of the ledger. I'll write boldly, in legible script. Ink, never pencil. I'll perform these duties with the exactitude of a diamond cutter.

(Pause.)

Happy?

(PARK stares at the checks.)

PARK: What is the Famine Fund?

FLO: It's my money, Park. I could spend it in worse ways. Some women buy oysters. Some buy satin sheets. Others, silk lingerie.

PARK: But not you.

FLO: No.

PARK: You buy children.

FLO: I do not *buy* children.

PARK: You rent children?

FLO: I *support* children.

PARK: If you're hell-bent on collecting babies, why waste time doing it through the mail? Just go outside and hail a cab. Drive up to the projects. Find an open window and wait under it.

FLO: Not funny, Park.

(PARK rifles through the checks.)

PARK: Sebdou, Burkina Faso. Maria, Ecuador. Moussi, Kenya. Jaime, Honduras. All yours?

FLO: They're mine, yes.

PARK: Is there a catalog? An 800 number?

FLO: Don't start, Park.

PARK: Late-night TV? That actress from the seventies. Coiffed and grinning, she glides through the dusty back roads of Sri Lanka, followed by a rainbow of children singing "Kumbaya" and proffering empty bowls. . . .

FLO: Those children are starving.

PARK: How many, total?

FLO: Twenty-two.

PARK: That's going to take a mighty large shoe, Flo.

FLO: So be it. We're "well heeled."

(FLO *smiles. She returns to her needlepoint.* PARK *pauses, devising a new angle on the same subject.*)

PARK: It's the worst kind of condescension.

FLO: Excuse me?

PARK: This "feel good" charity of yours.

(PARK *picks a check at random.*)

"Baku, Watbanaland." You don't *know* this child. You don't *know* Africa. Oh, to be fair you've read a few *National Geographic*s. "How to Build a Quonset Hut." You've seen a few grainy photos in the *Times*. You've been to a Broadway show, with men in kente cloth, harmonizing. You toss all these images into the Cuisinart that is your mind, add some sorry Polaroid of a bloated baby and—voilà! You, white woman, have accepted your burden. Unto you a son is born. Perhaps if one day you actually meet this Baku he will spit at your feet. Out of contempt for your ignorance. Your selfish appropriation.

FLO: What do we do, Park? Sit back and atrophy in the face of our own shortcomings? No. It is our responsibility to do more.

PARK: *Our?* Oh, no. Not *our.*

(PARK *crosses to the bar and pours a drink.*)

This is your project, not mine. I have hobbies of my own. Chess. Anagrams. This I leave to you.

FLO: Contrary to what your own experience might imply, the world is not some arid sphere. It's producing all the time. Squeezing out life. It is incumbent upon us to nurture what the world spawns.

(*Another brief pause.*)

Like it or not, Park, it is our duty to perpetuate the species. *Ourselves.* In whatever way we can.

PARK: I disagree.

FLO: Oh?

PARK: Nature monitors herself. We should not intervene.

FLO: That's inhumane.

PARK: Starvation. Infanticide. Cannibalism. These are Nature's tools.

FLO: We have a function, Park. We play a role. Her conscience. We are here to enforce an ethical code.

PARK: When a dog whelps and a resulting pup is deficient—born with two heads, perhaps, or obstructed bowels—the bitch instinctively devours it. Her eyes dripping with maternal woe, she takes the newborn in her jaws and begins to chew. That is mercy in its purest form.

FLO: We are not animals. The same rules do not apply.

PARK: To allow it to live—drooling across the floor, flopping to and fro—that is sadism. That, my dear, is moral bankruptcy.

FLO: You're being perverse.

PARK: We would do better, I think, if we had the courage . . . the strength of purpose . . . to eat our own.

(PARK *downs his drink. There is a long pause.*)

FLO: I have not walked across burning sand, or watched my skin shrivel from lack of drink, but I have lived here in this desolate place—these eight sterile rooms—I have felt your cold, dry breath on my neck, and that is my own profound poverty. I find solace in their pain. A sense of communion. In your parlance, a high return on my investment.

(PARK *tears up the canceled checks, slowly.*)

PARK: I will not have our savings spent to mock me.

FLO: I beg your pardon?

PARK: The account bears my surname. I refuse to be party to my own humiliation.

FLO: That's preposterous.

PARK: Every decimal point trumpets my inadequacies. Every zero, an implied insult.

FLO: It's not about you.

PARK: It doesn't take a doctor, some smug Sigmund Freud, to recognize your rather puny attempts to compensate for my deficiencies.

FLO: You're overreacting. This is nothing less than paranoia.

PARK: I'm closing the account.

FLO: But, Park—

PARK: Likewise the subject.

(FLO *stands, glares at him for a moment, and exits.* PARK *watches as the tattered checks flutter into the wastebasket. Blackout.*)

Scene 10

A pediatrics unit.

Milo's incubator has a white border that hides him from view. All around it, metal boxes, tubing, dials.

MARILYN *hovers over him like a lioness protecting her cub. She reads aloud from a fashion magazine.*

DASH, *in dark glasses and a leather jacket, paces.*

MARILYN: "Summer's synonymous with bangs, bobs, and pony-tails. You can spruce up your seasonal shag with barettes, color-ful clips, and hair-raising headbands guaranteed to garner glances, at the beach or in the boardroom—"

DASH: I'm casing the place. Exit locations. Police phones. Alarms.

MARILYN: Dash, quiet. I'm reading to the baby.

DASH: *Cosmo?*

MARILYN: It's my *voice*, asshole.

DASH *(To Milo.)*: Hey, li'l fella. Take a last look round this joint. To-morrow you're King of the Road.

(DASH exits.)

MARILYN: Milo, sweetheart. Your new daddy's got big plans. I hope you don't get carsick.

(PARK enters. He stands framed in the doorway.)

"Why not try a two-tone look—"

(PARK clears his throat. MARILYN turns to see him.)

What the hell are you doing here?

PARK: An overdue visit.

MARILYN: You got a pass?

PARK: From whom? That sleeping woman in the rotunda?

MARILYN: Dash is down the hall. He sees you here, talking to me now, and we are both fucked, big-time.

PARK: Milo's been preying on my mind, insinuating himself where he does not belong.

MARILYN: Milo's been nowhere but here, all by his lonesome, except for me.

PARK: Oh, no. He's come looming into my marriage, Marilyn. Like a torpedo.

MARILYN: Don't you go blaming him for things. He never ast to be born.

PARK: A year ago, decisions were made amid confusion . . . numbness . . . grief. Decisions that are, in fact, reversible. Which, in the clear light of day—

MARILYN: *Huh what?*

PARK: I need your consent.

MARILYN: What for?

PARK: I have a proposal. Know that I have the child's best interests at heart. *Our* best interests.

MARILYN: You sit here and squeeze his hand. You turn him over, so he don't get bedsores. Then you can waltz back in here with your proposal.

PARK: He is not your exclusive province. Would that he were.

MARILYN: You don't care if he lives or dies.

PARK: Quite the contrary.

MARILYN: You've never even looked him eye to eye.

PARK: Is that a dare, Marilyn?

MARILYN: Your own kid, and you never even bronzed his goddamn booties. You're a weak man, Mr. Stillman.

PARK: I would be happy . . . to look.

(PARK *doesn't move.*)

MARILYN: He's not fine china. He won't break.

(PARK *approaches the incubator; he stares at Milo.*)

He's got your nose.

PARK: Marilyn—

MARILYN: That got your pulse goin'.

(*A long pause.* PARK *is riveted. He doesn't move.*)

That all you gonna do? Stare him down?

(*Suddenly, with an expulsion of breath,* PARK *takes a step away from the incubator.*)

PARK: I thought we'd play patty-cake. London Bridge. I thought we'd share a stogie, and I'd tell him about girls.

MARILYN: You can touch him, at least.

PARK: Through the glass?

MARILYN: That's why they got these gloves.

PARK: That's thick plastic, Marilyn. When I touch him, he won't feel me. I won't feel him.

MARILYN: You won't know till you give it a try.

PARK: What will he do in response? Even a dog would wag its tail.

MARILYN: Sometimes he moves.

PARK: An involuntary spasm. A muscle tic. Nothing more.

MARILYN: You are a negative power person. Could you look at the plus side, maybe once? Milo got superior qualities. He don't talk down to me. He ain't two-faced. That kid—that *sweet* kid—he don't pull my chain. If I was you, I'd be proud to shake the little guy's hand.

PARK: He is an *object*, Marilyn. You can imagine a personality on his behalf, but that does not make him a human being.

(MARILYN *grins.*)

MARILYN: Like father, like son.

(*A pause.* MARILYN *rocks on her heels, victorious.* PARK *glares at her for a moment. Defiantly, he takes a step closer to the incubator.*)

PARK: Show me what to do. Well. I'm waiting.

MARILYN: One quick squeeze, then you are out of here.

(MARILYN *guides his hands into the gloves.*)

It's good for his circulation; gets the blood pumpin'.

(PARK *touches Milo.*)

PARK: He feels . . . he feels very much—

MARILYN: Yeah?

PARK: Like a child.

MARILYN: Tickle his chin. His mouth turns up. A sorta smile.

(PARK *does.*)

There ya go. Now tell me that kid's not laughin' somewhere inside. At us.

(PARK *is rooted to Milo, almost unable to speak.*)

PARK: Ahhh . . .

MARILYN: What?

PARK: His finger. It moved.

MARILYN: Told you so.

PARK: There was a reach. A reach toward me.

MARILYN: You're his father. He knows.

PARK: Look. It's curling. Around my thumb. He's holding on. He's gripping.

MARILYN: He's waited so long to meet you, he's not lettin' go now.

PARK: These aren't random stirrings. These are . . . *motor skills.* . . .

MARILYN: He's more than meets the eye, Mr. Stillman.

PARK: If I thought, Marilyn, for even a moment that he could understand . . . a *glimmer of recognition* . . . well then, I would . . .

MARILYN: You'd do what?

PARK: I would . . . tell him something.

MARILYN: What've you got to lose?

(PARK *leans over to address Milo.*)

PARK: I . . . ah . . .

(PARK *pulls back.*)

This is ridiculous.

MARILYN: Get ovah yourself. I talk his ear off.

(PARK *gestures to* MARILYN *for a moment of privacy. She rolls her eyes and steps away.* PARK *leans into the incubator; his voice is a whisper.*)

PARK: *I . . . am . . . so . . . sorry.*

(PARK *withdraws his hands from the gloves. He turns away from* MARILYN.)

MARILYN: Mr. Stillman? You O.K.?

PARK: I shouldn't intrude—

MARILYN: Wait—

PARK: The night nurse, she'll have my head.

MARILYN: You never came before. Why now?

PARK: Masochistic indulgence. A sudden whim. Dementia.

MARILYN: You want my consent? For what?

PARK: Oh. Yes. Your consent.

MARILYN: For what?

PARK: Knowing his condition, how very perishable, I would like your permission for . . . for . . .

MARILYN: Spit it out, Mr. Stillman.

(Pause.)

PARK: Visitation privileges.

MARILYN: Like, regular?

PARK: Think about it. Please.

MARILYN: After a whole year, you cannot walk in, *la-dee-da*, acting like you care. That just don't wash with me.

PARK: I'll understand if you decline.

(PARK exits. MARILYN looks after him to make sure he's gone.)

MARILYN: Holy fucking shit.

INTERCOM: "Dr. Goldfarb to the O.R. stat . . . Dr. Goldfarb to the O.R. stat . . ."

(DASH reenters, in stolen medical scrubs.)

DASH: Listen up.

MARILYN: You scared me.

DASH: Tomorrow. Oh ten hundred hours. Nurse Nancy goes on break. That's when we rock 'n' roll.

MARILYN: This is lunatic, Dash. This is a crime.

DASH: I'll pull the car up to the emergency dock. You unhook the kid.

MARILYN: Suppose he starts hyperventilating.

DASH: Babe, I got oxygen in the trunk. Eight units of saline. He's just gotta last the length of the hallway. You got the release?

(MARILYN *hands it to* DASH.)

Aw, fuck, Marilyn. Doctors, they don't sign their names with smiley faces. They do not dot their "*i*'s" with li'l hearts.

MARILYN: I'm sorry. I'm nervous.

DASH: You in this, Marilyn? You having second thoughts? Particular other influences which you should not be listening to?

MARILYN: Uh-uh.

DASH: I smell aftershave. *Expensive.*

MARILYN: My beauty magazines, they got samples.

DASH: For the last time, little miss. I'm Clyde. You Bonnie?

MARILYN: Suppose they put us up at the post office.

DASH: I gave us an alias. Mr. and Mrs. King. I made us married, so the cops don't get wise. You wanna do that? Get married?

MARILYN (*Offhand.*): Yeah, yeah.

(DASH *pulls* MARILYN *to him and kisses her forehead.*)

Promise we're gonna have our very own mortgage and a savings account. Promise it's gonna be *better*, not just *different.*

DASH: Cross my heart, hope to die.

MARILYN: Gimme one. Just to be sure.

DASH: In front of the baby?

MARILYN: He don't mind.

(DASH *wraps her in his arms and plants a major kiss.*)

DASH: Sorry, babe. Tunnel time.

(*He looks at* MARILYN; *her brow is furrowed.*)

Chill, Marilyn.

(*He exits.* MARILYN *starts to pray.*)

MARILYN: Dear Mary, Mother ah God, please don't be pissed off. Milo deserves better. I can't. I won't. I ain't leaving him behind. Make Mr. Stillman understand.

(*She crosses herself.*)

We are *all* your children; we make errors in our ways. Amen.

(*Blackout.*)

Scene 11

The Stillmans' living room.

PARK *plays solitaire.* FLO *pens a letter. She reads aloud for* PARK's *benefit. He ignores her.*

FLO: My dear Baku, *Salamalaikoum* to you and the Watbani. As the Field Office has undoubtedly told you, payment was stopped on my last five donations. Frantic to give, I went to the only source available to me—the nursery where I teach. These children, your compatriots, are saving their silver. Quarters from the tooth fairy. Lemonade stands. Each nickel, each dime hoarded in the hope that your father might purchase a new goat, that potable water might be transported to your compound. For you see, Baku, their ingenuousness has yet to curdle into cynicism. They have yet to pay the inordinately high cost of adult disappointment.

(FLO *checks to see if* PARK *is listening. He continues to flip cards.*)

How I yearn for a child like you.

(FLO *glances at* PARK *a second time to gauge his attention.*)

I invent stories.

(PARK *stops his cardplay.* FLO *smiles to herself.*)

In my dreams, of course, he is a model boy. A report card brimming with A's. Catcher for his Little League team. A member emeritus of the clean-plate club. One day he will, like all sons, be president. And—last but not least, and this is an absolute requisite—he is the apple of his father's eye.

(PARK *stands. A pause.*)

PARK: We go fishing. He watches me shave.

(FLO *closes her eyes and clasps her hands, as if in prayer.*)

FLO: Oh, God.

PARK: I stare at him some evenings as he splashes in the tub or lolls in sleep. His arms, lithe and pliable. The sculpted quality of each ear.

FLO: A widow's peak, perhaps.

PARK: His ten fingers. His ten toes.

FLO: *Yes.*

PARK: Each part so perfect. Each part so impossible.

(PARK *turns away from his wife. He wavers for a moment, then exits.* FLO, *overwhelmed, calls after him.*)

FLO: Park—

(*Offstage, a door slams. Blackout.*)

Scene 12

The lobby of a large investment firm. The genteel "ping" of roving elevators.

Piped-in music wafts past.

DASH *and* MARILYN *stand at a pay phone.*

MARILYN: No fucking way. Uh-uh. This is bogus, Dash. Let's wait till Friday. Pay day, whaddaya say? Money for the road. Brake fluid for the car, sodium chloride for the baby—

(DASH *holds up a quarter.*)

DASH: Yo, Marilyn. George Washington, he says you got three minutes to settle the score.

(DASH *puts the coin in the pay phone; he dials.*)

Ready. Set. Go.

(DASH *hands the receiver to* MARILYN. *She looks at it reluctantly, then brings it to her ear. She bites a nail. Brrring. Brrring. Lights rise in* PARK's *office.* PARK, *in suit and tie, stands at* MARILYN's *desk. He picks up the phone.*)

PARK: Stillman here.

MARILYN: G'morning. Guess who.

PARK: Marilyn. Where is the big hand? Where is the little hand?

MARILYN: So "Good afternoon."

(DASH *looms expectantly over her.*)

DASH: Tell him no funny stuff.

(MARILYN *covers the receiver with her palm.*)

MARILYN: Do you mind? You're breathing my air.

DASH: Tell him I'm on my way up.

(DASH *looks at her a beat, then exits.* MARILYN *speaks into the phone.*)

MARILYN: Mr. Stillman? I mailed your out-box, your in-box ain't in yet, and I quit.

(*Pause.*)

PARK: Excuse me?

MARILYN: I broke the sublease on the condo.

PARK: Oh no, you don't.

MARILYN: And I . . . aw, Christ . . . I took the Camaro back to the lot.

PARK: There are procedures, protocol, otherwise chaos. Where are you?

MARILYN: An "undisclosed location."

PARK: I know that Muzak, Marilyn. The lobby, yes? I'll come down. We'll do lunch. That Italian place you like so much, with the plastic statuary and the fronds.

MARILYN (*Trying to wind it up.*): Thanks for everything, and thanks for nothin'.

PARK: Life without pay-per-view? Life without aroma therapy? I give you two weeks, maximum.

MARILYN: I'll surprise ya, Mr. Stillman.

PARK: You do not walk out. This is absurd, the telephone. Come upstairs.

MARILYN: I gotta go—

PARK: What about Milo?

MARILYN: He's in good hands.

PARK: Whose?

MARILYN: Dash got him rigged in the backseat.

PARK: In the car?

MARILYN: We got a cardiovascular pump and a little egg-crate mattress—

PARK: You have placed a terminal infant in the backseat of an automobile?

MARILYN: It's a Buick LeSabre.

PARK: I don't care if it's a fucking Corniche!

MARILYN: I hold him in my lap, I cushion the road bumps.

PARK: You can't just stroll out with the baby on your back! You've got no income, no health coverage—

MARILYN: I'm cashing the Christmas Club. That was for him, not me.

PARK: You won't find another job that takes Milo so utterly into consideration. You will sling burgers, Marilyn, you will sell face paint door to door—

MARILYN: He's not your baby anymore, ya understand?

PARK: Milo is my dubious legacy to the world, and I will have him.

MARILYN: I gave your half to Dash.

PARK: I will notify the doctors—

MARILYN: He deserves a backyard, Mr. Stillman—

PARK: Reckless endangerment—

MARILYN: And a bassinet—

PARK: Possibly even abuse—

MARILYN: And a hobby horse!

PARK: Damn it, Marilyn!

MARILYN: A normal life—

PARK: He is not a normal child!

MARILYN: Don't you be yelling at me!

PARK: *Last night, Marilyn!*

MARILYN *(Her voice breaking.)*: I just wanna say, and I mean this, what happened with us, that's between you and God now. I hope He forgives you. More'n that, I hope you forgive yourself.

PARK: When you resettle, we will arrange for a post-office box, and I will send funds.

MARILYN: Forget me.

PARK: From a trust in Milo's name—

MARILYN: Forget Milo.

PARK: Cash, then. I will send you cash! Unmarked bills! Tell me what to do and I will swear by it. . . .

(A clicking sound from the phone.)

THE TELEPHONE: "Please deposit five cents for the next three minutes or your call will be terminated."

MARILYN: Aw, fuck.

PARK: A nickel. God damn you! Put a nickel in the fucking phone. . . . Marilyn? HELLO?

(A dial tone, MARILYN hangs up. She wipes her eyes on her sleeve. Lights on the pay phone fade. PARK smashes the phone repeatedly against the desk. It goes dead. He lets it hang off the hook. DASH enters the office. He's carrying an empty cardboard box.)

Well, look who's here. Back from the tolls. Fresh off the highway.

DASH: I come to clean out Marilyn's things.

PARK: We have a custodial staff, paid to attend to such matters. To wash away our somewhat transient employees . . .

DASH: I come for her valuables.

(DASH *starts to fill the cardboard box with knickknacks and supplies from* MARILYN's *desk.*)

PARK: I can't allow it. Office property.

DASH: She gave me a list. Her hockey mug, her Bon Jovi tapes, one gold bracelet. These things, they are not "office property."

PARK: You put her up to this, didn't you?

(DASH *continues to empty the desk. He ignores* PARK.)

The phone call downstairs. Her knight in shining armor, yes?

DASH: Look, asshole, I know your species. Slick as silk on the outside, but inside you're toxic, man. You are not immune to permutations in the biological world. To disaster. Look at me, all denim and grease. But inside my neurons are numero uno.

(DASH *overturns a drawer into the box.*)

PARK: Let me tell you something, friend. Pal. There is no glory in cleaning up another man's mistakes.

DASH *(Holding up a stapler.)*: This her stapler or yours?

PARK: You won't find redemption in another man's sins.

DASH *(Again, more insistent.)*: Is this her stapler or yours?

PARK: I'm not in your way. I make no claims. I am simply tending to the mess I made. My little spill.

DASH: Answer me.

PARK: I can see it now, the three of you, headed west; the Good

Samaritan and his somewhat instant family. The fun lasts a week, maybe two, then she gets grumpy, cramps maybe, and at the next Motor Inn she wants twin instead of queen size. You're left alone in the dark, cradling poor Milo, changing his bags until the tubes start to tighten about your neck. What happens to charity then, friend?

DASH: Ten seconds till I shove this stapler up your ass. Ten . . . Nine . . . Eight . . . Seven . . . Six . . .

PARK: Go ahead! Why not? Take it all!

(PARK *pulls drawers from the desk, dumping the contents into the box.*)

DASH: Whoa, mister! Hey, mister! Hands off!

PARK: Take the blotter, the nameplate, her fucking snooze alarm! But leave me one thing. Please.

(*Pause.*)

I saw him. I *felt* him.

DASH: Too little, too late, "Still-man." We all know about you. What you can do. What you have done.

(*Pause.*)

God, mister. You oughtta be careful what you touch.

(*Blackout.*)

Scene 13

The sound of a television in the darkness.

THE TELEVISION: This is WPQR, Sunshine Television. The following paid programming does not reflect the views of this station's management, affiliates, employees, or advertisers.

(*A pause, and then a familiar celebrity voice.*)

PENELOPE WAX: Good morning. My name is Penelope Wax. Many of you already know me as the free-spirited Vera Dent in the hit series *LoveQuest 99*. Off-camera, I play a very different role: celebrity chairperson for Bulimics Anonymous.

(Lights rise to reveal the Stillmans' kitchen. It is smartly furnished; the table is heavy oak, the Bentwood chairs have paisley cushions, and the refrigerator is jumbo-sized. FLO wears a tasteful house robe and petit-point slippers. First, she slices oranges in half with a knife. Then—with all her might—she squeezes them into juice. Her shoulders pivot with the motion of her wrist. On the countertop is a small TV.)

We all know the lure of the last piece of almond torte. The silent beckoning of Grandma's lemon chiffon. But for some women bingeing is a constant obsession. Mary W. is a sophomore at an exclusive private school on Manhattan's affluent Upper East Side:

(In a voice-over, the testimony of "MARY W.")

MARY W.: "I started purging when I was still a preteen. After every meal. My friends had nicknamed me 'Old Faithful.' One night, I collapsed in the middle of a party. Doctor said it was malnutrition. That's when I knew I needed help."

(The refrigerator door opens. YOBO MUNDE steps out of the appliance and into the room, softly. FLO does not notice his entrance. He approaches her from behind.)

PENELOPE WAX: Mary had the foresight to contact Bulimics Anonymous. Thanks to counseling she received at our Manhattan outreach clinic, she's now a healthy, happy size 5.

(FLO senses the presence of a stranger in the room. She doesn't move; the tension is palpable. Hesitantly, she clicks off the TV. Gently, YOBO MUNDE reaches out and takes her arm. She bristles. In the distance, a cacophony of drums.)

YOBO MUNDE: In Watbanaland, we have no closets of winter. Your boxes of milk. Your food, wrapped in silver skins. In Watbanaland, we have only heat. Heat to burn water from the body. Heat to burn blood. Heat to turn a child into bone and leather.

(Slowly, FLO turns to face him.)

My wife Modwabbi. She eats only sand and locusts. She has lost her hair and her teeth from hunger. Still, she knows that together we must chisel a future. And so she drops babies like fruit. From her ass, babies. From her mouth, babies. They grow on her back, off her arms, they dangle from her knees. I cut them off her with my scythe, like I cut branches from a tree. As soon as I cut, she sprouts more. My children, some of them are small, the size of my fist. I name them all. Once, together, these words made a family. Now they form a death song.

(YOBO sings.)

Todwana, Aku, Ishiri, Ejabo, Mudeeb, Katwabo, Maldab, Nogobo.

(He stops singing.)

They curl first in my arms, then they curl in the sun like burned leaves. I have one son left: Baku. Baku lies on the floor. Baku doesn't move. When I hold Baku up to the sky, I see light shining through his ribs. Like his brothers, Baku shall soon turn to sand.

(FLO tries to speak, but the words won't come. YOBO takes her hands in his, with sudden urgency.)

In your vessels, pomegranate. In your cauldrons, meat. Your silos stink with the smell of rotting corn. You hunt for sport, then throw the kill away. When you starve, it is for vanity. *You must help us!* Seedlings, to turn cracked ground into a garden. Pumps to draw rivers from beneath the desert floor. These are yours to share. My son must carry us into tomorrow. My son must be stronger than the earth.

(FLO *nods, tight-lipped, almost trembling.*)

I won't harm you. I will only talk. We'll give words to each other, yes?

(*Suddenly* FLO *grabs* YOBO MUNDE's *face and kisses him long and slow. Her legs wrap about his waist. The drums crescendo. Blackout.*)

ACT TWO

Scene 1

FLO *sits high on her stool, holding a picture book. She wears a few African bracelets and an elephant-hair necklace. She is quite obviously pregnant.*

FLO: "So Mr. Dingle pulled up his bootstraps and said to the cabbage, 'My, oh my but you're leafy and green!' The cabbage rolled its eyes and shook its head and moaned its cabbage moan. . . ."

(In the distance, the remote roar of a giant cat. The light turns a blazing white. FLO *is distracted, then continues reading.)*

"Mr. Dingle had never been in the mysterious garden before, and he had never heard a cabbage wail. . . ."

(The rattle of drums. FLO *stops cold.)*

Shh. Class. Listen.

*(*FLO *closes the book.)*

Do you remember the stick baby? That's right. Baku. And where is Baku from? It's a long word. Ruthie, yes. Watbanaland. Ruthie gets a gold star. As we sit in air-conditioned comfort, reading this colorful book, diverting ourselves from the world outside, what do you suppose Baku is doing? Tending the goats? Maybe, if there are goats to tend. Grinding millet? Perhaps, if the crops did not burn. Suppose we could invite Baku to be here, with us, in the nursery. Suppose we could share snack time with Baku. We'd give him a napkin, and a big, tall glass of orange juice. Yes. Fresh-squeezed. And what would Baku do? He'd drink that juice right down, to ward off scurvy, to fatten his brittle bones—his bones like thermometers, his mouth like a gaping wound. He'd suck it down fast, because back home, in

Watbanaland, the land is parched and unable to bring forth fruit. When we look into his eyes, his round, saucer eyes, what do we see? A vast, inner cavern of want. Want so large it terrifies. A hunger so rapacious that if we don't hold fast to the furniture, we, too, shall be sucked under and devoured.

(FLO *stretches out her hand.*)

Ruthie. Mrs. Stillman is shaking. Hold Mrs. Stillman's hand.

(*A faraway cry.* FLO *closes her eyes.*)

Did you hear that? On the wind, across the sand, a cry. Another baby being born.

(FLO *cups her rounded belly. Two sharp intakes of breath. She sits, stonestill. The sound dies away. The lights are restored,* FLO *sighs deeply, then opens her eyes.*)

Where were we?

(*She opens the book and resumes reading.*)

" 'Good gracious!' cried Mr. Dingle to the cabbage. 'I never heard such a noise!' With that, the cabbage only groaned more loudly, so the carrots quivered and the rutabaga shook with fear. . . ."

(*Blackout.*)

Scene 2

PARK's *office.*

It is late. A single lamp illuminates PARK's *face as he speaks on the telephone.*

PARK: Yes. I'd like to inquire regarding the status of a particular file. . . . A child, barely a year and a half old, reported missing some months ago. . . . Milo Klepowski . . . His name, not mine . . . A relative? No. No relation. A friend, yes. I am his friend. No. Not a friend. A benefactor. A concerned citizen. I saw his face on a milk carton, and I haven't been able to sleep. A cousin, perhaps. No. His doctor. I am his doctor. Wait. Hello?

(Blackout.)

Scene 3

A motel somewhere in the Midwest. The bedspread matches the art print on the wall.

A bureau drawer is open, forming a makeshift crib for Milo.

DASH lies on the bed. It vibrates beneath him.

MARILYN stares at DASH and combs her hair with vigor. She tries to get a rise out of him.

MARILYN: Superman. Lone Ranger.

(The bed stops vibrating. DASH inserts another quarter.)

　　Fucking Lancelot.

DASH: You want me to pound your head or what?

MARILYN: Five months, I haven't peed in the same toilet twice. That's not what you promised, Dash, that's not *stability*.

DASH: Where the hell are we?

MARILYN: Can't you read? It's on the postcards.

DASH: Springfield what? Iowa? Kansas? Nebraska? Name one state without a Springfield, I'll butter your feet and lick 'em clean.

MARILYN: Look in the phone book.

DASH: All we got is Gideon.

MARILYN: You shoulda followed the map.

DASH: The map is your job.

MARILYN: I can't follow *squiggles*.

DASH: Dumb fuck.

MARILYN: Suppose the map was wrinkled, which it is! We're not even driving down roads; we're driving down goddamn wrinkles!

DASH: We drove eight hundred miles down a *wrinkle*?

MARILYN: So?

DASH: So?

MARILYN: Weren't you watching the road?

DASH: Sometimes.

MARILYN: *Sometimes?*

DASH: I kept one eye on the rearview, on junior. I dint wanna take the potholes too fast.

MARILYN: Check the lot.

DASH: Huh?

MARILYN: The license plates.

(DASH *bolts up from the bed and exits. From offstage, he yells back.*)

DASH: Colorado. Texas. Arkansas.

(*He reenters, fuming.*)

It's a fucking motel, Marilyn.

MARILYN: Call the desk.

DASH: No way.

MARILYN: Why not?

DASH: Excuse me, can we have some extra ice for the bucket, and oh, by the way, what frigging state are we in?

MARILYN: What, you think you have a reputation to protect here? An image to uphold? Mr. Radar. Mr. Cartographer.

DASH: You call.

MARILYN: I gotta feed the baby.

(MARILYN *plops a suitcase on the bed and opens it. As they talk, she pulls a hammer and some nails from the suitcase. She pounds three nails into the wall above the bureau.*)

DASH: You wanna know where we are?

(DASH *opens the drapes and stares outside.*)

A desert. Look. Sand. Nothing's growin'.

(*He pulls the drapes shut.*)

I ain't used to this.

MARILYN: You said, "Come on." You said, "Be a household."

DASH: We're engaged, aren't we? I gave you a ring.

MARILYN: That is not a ring, Dash; that is a pull tab. Offa light-beer can. That don't count. That's no band o' gold.

DASH: It's temporary.

MARILYN: I thought I was gonna wind up with a honest-to-God rock. A walk-in closet, and window treatments. What've I got instead, eh? I got a hundred tiny shampoo bottles and a "Do Not Disturb" hanging from my rearview mirror.

DASH: I got a bitch who nags at seventy-two r.p.m.

MARILYN: And Milo. What's he got, eh?

DASH: You and me, baby. On a string.

MARILYN: I never ast you, I never begged. You ast *me*, you begged *me*.

DASH: Yeah, yeah . . .

MARILYN: Look at me. Who broke into the hospital? Who stole his prescriptions?

DASH: I know what I did.

MARILYN: Who ran down the hallway with a backpack full of baby?

DASH: I nailed my own hands to my own cross.

MARILYN: I had a job. I had light typing, and my own phone line. I had big, fat checks slipped under the table. I had Milo under glass. Not underfoot. I liked visiting hours, Dash. They don't last a lifetime.

(MARILYN *retrieves two liquid bags from a Styrofoam cooler. One is filmy, and one is clear. Each has its own IV tube. She snaps on rubber gloves.*)

DASH: There's certain kinds of bats, born widdout eyeballs. Instead they got supersonic sound waves. Better than your normal pupil, ten times the accuracy. Milo's like that.

MARILYN: Milo's like Milo.

DASH: So what if he ain't got sight or sound or taste. So what if he ain't got a normal head-full. He's got gravitational pull. You, me, and Stillman—we're planets revolving round him. He holds us there by force of will, going in circles around him, like he was the sun.

MARILYN: We never shoulda run, Dash.

DASH: We're not running away. We're breaking force fields. We're ripping the Milky Way apart at the seams. You want a piece of cake, you go to the bakery. You want to rearrange the planets, you stick with me.

(MARILYN *stands and hangs the three bags on the corresponding nails. She kneels down beside* MILO *and gently attaches the IV tubes.*)

I'm going out. Find a clinic.

MARILYN: It's six o'clock in the A.M.

DASH: What, you want us to starve?

MARILYN: Can't you get yourself a real job?

DASH: Fugitives do not settle down. Fugitives do not work real jobs.

MARILYN: You swore to me: one day, "highway patrol."

DASH: I dint know you had a *stopwatch*.

MARILYN: It's no better'n being a whore, selling off your body fluids.

DASH: It's charity work.

MARILYN: A few skin mags and a Dixie Cup. *Thwap, thwap, thwap.* You're a real humanitarian.

(DASH *flexes in the mirror.*)

DASH: It's more than that, Marilyn. Women cry out for my stuff like junkies cry for crack. Men write checks 'cause I got what they don't.

MARILYN: It's babies they want, Dash. Not you.

DASH: My gourmet genes taking root in bellies from Schenectady to Nome.

MARILYN: You got primo DNA, and for what? It's like God took a diamond and hid it inside a shit pile. No job. No home. No lawn to mow, no hatchback, nothing.

DASH: Yo. Don't you forget.

MARILYN: Forget *what?*

DASH: I pulled on my red cape and my slippers, and I swooped down and rescued you. Like it or not, I rescued you.

(Blackout.)

Scene 4

The bedroom of the Stillmans' apartment.

PARK *is propped up in bed with pillows. His glasses are tipped on his nose. He looks past the top ridge of his book to stare directly at* FLO.

FLO *is on the floor at the foot of the bed, doing breathing exercises.*

PARK: The milkman.

FLO: No.

PARK: The postman, perhaps. A "Special Delivery."

FLO: "Mail carrier." Female.

PARK: Well, then. Some knobby-kneed john from TV Repair. A low-hanging tool belt and a gift for mending broken tubes.

FLO: The television is not broken. The television is above reproach.

PARK: Maybe it's the product of a furtive, late-night tryst in a hospital laboratory. Flo, in velvet and pearls, slipping out to meet a test tube on the sly.

FLO: Mmm. Yes. The beaker in the red carnation.

PARK: Stop the presses. Hold the phone. A scorching summer day. The Lincoln Tunnel. You needed change. In the toll booth a strapping young buck with government-endorsed genes. Fairly throbbing out of his uniform. A smile, a wink, a few quick thrusts, waiting for the green to flash and the gate to rise. That's it. It has to be. Poetic justice. The circle completes itself.

(Pause.)

Well? Am I warm? Am I cold?

FLO: You are frigid, Park.

PARK: Then who?

FLO: An African chieftain. With a certain majesty, a mythic resonance, he lay in wait for me one morning in the ice box. One foot in the vegetable crisper, the other in the egg tray. There— on the kitchen table, oranges bouncing on the parquet like rubber balls—he plundered me. Correction. I plundered him.

PARK: Sorry, Flo. Too preposterous. You lack the necessary light touch for this particular parlor game.

FLO: You've given this substantial thought. Should I be flattered?

PARK: We won't keep it. We'll wrap it in a pillowcase and leave it on a doorstep. We'll slip it through the bars at the zoo.

FLO: I've hired a decorator. To convert your study.

PARK: We cannot have an infant in this house, Flo. It is not a fit climate. We have not secured our cleaning solvents, or put a fence at the top of the stairs. Have you inspected the ceiling for asbestos? Have you read the fine print on the Similac? Poison often lurks in seemingly impotent places. What about me, Flo? I might be a very dangerous place for a child.

FLO: Your concerns are misplaced. Worse, they are vain. Insinuating yourself. Your contagion. This child has nothing to do with you.

PARK: Then you cannot expect me to welcome it into my home. To coddle and feed it, as a house cat might nurse an orphaned jaguar. I know the end of that story, Flo.

FLO: You're frightened.

PARK: Yes.

FLO: Of a baby.

PARK: Bingo.

FLO: I suppose it's natural. You've never felt the flush of father-hood. You've never held a newborn infant in your arms.

PARK: No. Never.

FLO: They seem exotic.

PARK: Very.

FLO: Beyond your reach.

PARK: Far.

FLO: It's comic. Like fearing your own shadow.

(Pause.)

PARK: There is one.

FLO: Yes?

PARK: A child with whom I have had contact. A relationship, of sorts.

FLO *(Heartened.)*: Well, now. A place to start.

PARK: My last secretary, Marilyn, up-by-the-roots Marilyn, fly-by-night Marilyn, she has a baby. It's the saddest thing. Anen-cephalic. Stem but no cerebrum. His heart pumps, his lungs inflate, but to no discernible end. He will never walk. He will never whistle. He will never stare at a mirror in recognition of himself.

(Pause. PARK *edges toward the truth.)*

I saw him once. He lay encased in glass. Velcro tabs on his arms. His mouth taped full of tubes. Trapped inside himself. A victim of his own limitations. Our children, some say, are the truest re-flections of ourselves. And if that's so, well . . . *good God.*

(Pause.)

Imagine producing a child like that. The rage you would feel. Against your own body. Against nature. The unforgivable things it would make you do.

(Long pause.)

FLO: You want to terrorize me.

PARK: You miss the point.

FLO: If I were about to board a plane, you'd recount tales of airline disaster. The faulty wing. The undescended mask.

PARK: No, Flo please, I—

FLO: I will give birth to this child. It will push from me, then stand on its own feet, and one day, like all children, it will outgrow you, it will surpass you, it will continue into space and time beyond you, and it will have the strength to silence you.

PARK: You're not out of the woods yet. Fetal intrauterine infections. Phocomelia. Abruptio placentae. The fetus could strangle itself during birth. Crib death.

(Pause.)

A million miracles just waiting to happen.

(A speedy blackout. Lights rise almost instantly on the following scene.)

Scene 5

The Stillmans' bedroom. PARK *has disappeared.*

FLO *now sits on the bed, her legs parted, her back arched, prepared to give birth.* YOBO MUNDE *towers over her.*

Drums in the distance. They rumble, louder. More insistent.

YOBO MUNDE: In Watbanaland, a child born without breath is a gift from Mawu to a starving people.

(YOBO *raises his hand above* FLO's *body; sand trickles from his grip. It falls in a thin strand over her womb, between her legs.*)

Children who live claw the ground for food. They sever their tongues and swallow. We feed them cloth from our backs. To quench their thirst, we drink blood and tears and spit into their mouths. Soon there is nothing left to sustain us. Nothing but the sour fruit of a woman's belly. What is savage? To watch, helpless, as a child dies, or to use what Mawu has given? A baby born without breath is a night without hunger. The grief of the mother is great, and so we must tie her down. We think only of tomorrow, and not of the task which lies before us. If we forget our purpose, sorrow will tear the knife from our hands.

(YOBO *takes a piece of rope from around his own neck and ties* FLO's *hands above her body.*)

We take the body, small and wrapped in muslin. Though we are dressed in mourning, we stoke the fire and fill our pots with blood.

(FLO *lurches to life. She cringes, her eyes wide. Fast blackout. Again, the lights rise quickly on the following scene.*)

Scene 6

The Stillmans' bedroom.

No sign of YOBO. *In his place,* PARK.

FLO, *no longer pregnant, sits on the edge of the bed.* PARK *massages her shoulders.*

FLO: Did you hear something?

PARK: Hmm?

FLO: A child.

PARK: A Valium, Flo?

FLO: It's crying.

PARK: There was no child.

FLO: It wants comfort.

PARK: Should we telephone the doctor again? So he can remind you
of the outcome? So he can correct your . . . misconception?

FLO: I'm not dreaming, Park. It's a sound I know. It's my profession.
I am trained to recognize the signs of a child in distress.

PARK: I read an article once, in a health magazine, by an amputee. A
heliport, a defective blade. One of those stories. He had his left
leg removed from its hip socket. Several operations. A slow recovery, learning to walk on fiberglass. Still, the most unsettling as-
pect of the experience was the phantom recurrence of his absent
limb. At night he would awaken and feel the damaged leg, bleed-
ing and swollen in the bed, annexed to his trunk. Worse still, the
itching of an invisible toe. This would send him into paroxysms
of grief. The accident occurred some twenty years ago. Still, the
author keeps his shoes lined neatly in his closet, in pairs.

(PARK *kneads, harder.* FLO *winces. Blackout. Lights up onstage.*)

Scene 7

The Stillmans' bedroom. A baby crib stands in a pool of light.

FLO *is now crouched on the bed, facing* YOBO MUNDE.

YOBO MUNDE *is perched on the headboard. He cradles a calabash.*

Once again, PARK *has vanished.*

YOBO MUNDE: We take your child, born without breath. We walk
far from the compound, away from the eyes of the women and

the young. We tear limbs from a sacred tree and spark them. We have no need for water. We boil our tears.

(The baby crib begins to blaze.)

We do not pray for it. We do not name it. The flames lick the copper; we pray for you. The vapors rise sweet like honey; we give you the name "mother." We pour the nectar, rich from your womb, into gourds. We journey home. The wind fills our footprints with sand. Baku lies in straw. He does not move. I bring the gourd to his lips. The sweetness of your child fills his mouth. It runs down his cheeks and into the fissures of the earth below. I stroke his throat. He swallows. His eyes open. They shine like polished beads.

*(*YOBO *puts the calabash down. He stretches his arms to* FLO*; she clasps his hands.)*

You give life. Know that you give life.

(The crib continues to burn. Blackout.)

Scene 8

The living room of the Stillmans' apartment.

PARK *sits at the small desk. He is disheveled. Before him, a stack of paper. A bottle of ink.*

He writes furiously.

PARK: Dear Flo,

They say even the most ardent sadist can still be driven deaf by screams. And so I am writing you this note. For months, you implored me to give you a child. Surprise, surprise. I already have one. His name is Milo. He lies between us in the bed at night. I reach out to touch you, and he bites my hand. He is as misshapen and voracious as our marriage. In the nursery, you are surrounded by perfection. Ripped from the labels of Zwieback and Gerber—gorgeous children, kissed by God. I could not give you less. I feared creating another monster; instead, I became one. You attempted pregnancy without me. Ha-ha. Hysterical. When there was no resulting baby, you cried into a blue linen handkerchief. I saved that handkerchief. Behind a closed door, Bartók blaring, I cried, too. Our tears mingled in the fabric, the first time we have mixed fluids in years. I have a final and persistent fantasy. One evening—tonight, perhaps— you will walk into the room, ready as always to be hoisted on the rack. Instead, I will guide you gently to a chair. On my knees, I will divulge everything. Perhaps—just once, God, grant me this, please—our lives will explode in violence. I, tearing at your skirts, heaving sobs; you, bruising me with your fists. Primitive, yes, but not devious. In the end, of course, you will forgive me. Thus purged, I will once again be free. Able to look at you. To touch you in the dark. You asked once if I loved you. I have that question documented on tape, in our safe-deposit box. The answer? With great pain.

(FLO *enters. She is dressed in her house robe and slippers.* PARK *puts down his pen.*)

FLO: Coming to bed?

PARK: Is that a question or a pointless request?

FLO: Rote, Park. Nothing more. What are you writing?

PARK: The usual. A suicide note. A letter to your parents in Greenwich, requesting ransom.

FLO: Don't be long. I'll be asleep, I promise.

(FLO *exits.* PARK *picks up the pen again and resumes.*)

PARK: I cannot show you this letter. That is my weakness, that is my flaw. Like so much in our relationship, like so much in my life, I'm left to devour it alone, where it can fester, a hidden toxin, the poison I inflict in tiny drops upon the world.

(PARK *eats the letter. Blackout.*)

Scene 9

A hospital corridor. Plastic seats in primary colors.

MARILYN *and* DASH *sit side by side.* MARILYN *wears a new sundress.* DASH *wears the official uniform of the Highway Patrol.*

INTERCOM: "Dr. Marion to Pediatrics . . . Dr. Marion to Pediatrics . . ."

MARILYN: I gave him a playpen. I gave him wallpaper, with little ducks.

DASH: He was a good kid, a primo kid, only he wasn't born with the right batteries.

MARILYN: I gave him a rattle. A stroller. *I gave him all those things.* And for what? He still couldn't say "Mama."

DASH: Regular stuff don't make him a regular baby.

MARILYN: It's our fault. Too many months on the road. Dragging him all across kingdom come.

DASH: Bullshit, Marilyn. He had it *good.* Babies like him, they don't live this long. Not outside the womb. Three months, tops. Milo was shy two years. He was some kinda record.

MARILYN: Sticking him in plywood drawers, hanging his tubes offa picture hooks—

DASH: They got doctors flying in from Boston. They're gonna take pictures, write him up. He was a champion.

(Pause.)

Me and Milo. We're medical history.

MARILYN: I wish I was very young. Or very old. Anything but this moment.

DASH: Babe, right now, for us, this is fucking *creation*. We got a loan from the bank, new linoleum. I got my own motorcycle from the Highway Department. We're moving, Mare, a rung at a time. Pretty soon, a cedar fence. Burglar alarms.

MARILYN: Silk paper can still catch fire, Dash. It still burns.

DASH: The future, babe. That's all I'm saying.

(Pause.)

MARILYN: I want children. Wall-to-wall.

(MARILYN smiles wanly; she squeezes DASH's hand.)

Now you got a proper job, no more clinics. No more Dixie Cups.

DASH: Don't you worry, little miss. I'm saving up my prize-winning baby bullets. You and me, we're gonna have a thoroughbred.

MARILYN: Kid's not even born, he's got a million brothers. I'll bet by now your kids could fill a stadium.

DASH: What can I say, eh? I made my mark.

(Pause.)

So, ah. Marilyn. Paperwork.

MARILYN: Do we hafta?

DASH: Yeah.

(MARILYN picks up a hospital clipboard. She looks at the attached forms.)

MARILYN: He's got good eyes. They should keep his eyes.

DASH: Just sign the form.

MARILYN: His heart, too. For some little girl, maybe.

DASH: Sure.

(MARILYN *signs.*)

MARILYN: Some kids grow up, go to school, get jobs. Doctors cure people. Teachers teach. Milo, he'll give back, too. Just by being born, he'll give back.

DASH: He'll go on living in different bodies. Milo's eyes, still looking out at the world, blinking. Milo's heart, still ticking. Four or five different kids all sharing the same soul. They're satellites. He's mission control.

MARILYN: I'd like a lock of hair. You think they'd do that for me?

DASH: I'll ask.

MARILYN: To wear, maybe. To press in a book.

DASH: I'll cut it myself.

(MARILYN *stands, resolved.*)

MARILYN: I gotta tell Mr. Stillman.

DASH: Put it in a letter.

MARILYN: I hafta do it in person, Dash.

DASH: You ain't goin' nowhere. I just bought you a bungalow. I just gave you blue-ribbon babies. You ain't goin' back.

MARILYN: Watch me.

DASH: You let 'em take the good stuff outta Milo. Let 'em send Stillman the rest. All wrapped up in a big box with a red bow.

(MARILYN *slaps* DASH, *hard.*)

God, baby, I'm sorry.

MARILYN: You big, stupid fuck.

DASH: But he gave you money. I turned over my life.

MARILYN: It's hard for you. I know that.

DASH: "Till death do us part."

MARILYN: I said it, too. Remember?

DASH: Look at your finger.

MARILYN: Dash—

DASH: Look at your goddamn hand.

(MARILYN *tries to hide her hand behind her back;* DASH *grabs it. A ring glistens.*)

That ain't no pull tab. You know where that's from? Deep inside the ground. From a mine. In Africa. That didn't come in no six-pack.

MARILYN: If some blind baby sees, that's Stillman and me. If some baby gets new kidneys, it's him and me, not you. I may not like it, you may not like it, but that's science. I gotta give Stillman that.

DASH: No, you don't.

MARILYN: You set me free; I gotta set him free. Almost three years, I was yoked to that man. Now I'm busting up planets, Dash. It's me cutting cords.

(*Blackout.*)

Scene 10

The Stillmans' living room.

MARILYN *sits on the sofa.* FLO *stands behind her.*

DASH *looms at the door.*

FLO: Marilyn Klepowski.

MARILYN: "King" now.

FLO: Someday, I knew we'd meet.

MARILYN: All those years on the telephone.

FLO: Person-to-person but never face-to-face.

MARILYN: You dint come to the Christmas parties.

FLO: I'm private by nature.

DASH: She don't want coffee. No finger sandwiches, no hors d'oeuvres. Do I make myself clear?

MARILYN: Dash.

DASH: I drove her three thousand miles. In a new car that I purchased, on fuel from a gas card registered in my name. We provide for ourselves now.

(DASH *takes* MARILYN *by the shoulders.*)

Yo, Marilyn. When you see the man, what's the dish?

MARILYN: Now?

DASH: I wanna hear it.

MARILYN: "Hello, Mr. Stillman. Dash bought me a highboy and a pink chandelier."

DASH: And what else?

MARILYN: "And he bought me a house to put 'em in."

DASH: And the part I wrote out, on the napkin?

MARILYN: "And we're gonna have an army of perfect children. And their children will bear children, and their children will bear children, and their children will bear children, till the end of time."

(DASH *kisses* MARILYN*'s forehead.*)

DASH: Beautiful.

MARILYN: What now, you want it in pig Latin?

DASH: You tell him one more thing.

MARILYN: Huh, what?

DASH: You tell him I got my outsides matching my insides.

(DASH *turns to* FLO.)

I always wanted to see your husband's apartment, ma'am. I wanted to see what volume and quality of stuff a man would purchase to compensate for that which is lacking within himself.

(DASH *surveys the room.*)

You got nice chairs.

MARILYN: Leave us alone, O.K.?

DASH: Ten minutes, then I start with the horn.

(DASH *exits.*)

FLO: Park said you left suddenly. That you eloped. Did you elope?

MARILYN: Sort of.

FLO: And your husband.

MARILYN: Highway patrol.

FLO: Tell me. When he speaks to you, do your eyes meet? At night, does he touch you?

MARILYN: Excuse me?

FLO: Sometimes in the morning, at the basin, your former employer would brush against me while reaching for the toothpaste. It was excruciating. Was Park ever cruel to you, Marilyn?

MARILYN: Once or twice. Yeah. Often.

FLO: He is no longer cruel. That's something, at least.

MARILYN: I tried the office first. They said Mr. Stillman was, like, "indisposed." Is this a bad time?

FLO: Why are you here?

MARILYN: Loose ends.

FLO: Perhaps you have come in hopes of extorting severance pay. Well, Mr. Stillman is no longer solvent.

MARILYN: I got no claims. Not anymore.

FLO: As you know, Park had no biological children. He was, however, a foster father of some renown. Children are notoriously expensive. They will eat you alive.

MARILYN: Did he talk to you?

FLO: He is my husband.

MARILYN: But did he *talk* to you?

FLO: No.

(Pause.)

MARILYN: Let me see him.

FLO: My husband is ill.

MARILYN: I'm not leaving; I'm furniture.

FLO: He is well beyond "indisposed." He is, in fact, disposable.

MARILYN: Ten hours a day, five days a week, I had his voice on a Dictaphone shoved up my ear. That is *intimate*, lady. Me and him were stuck together like glue, like a coupla Siamese twins, there was flesh and blood between us. You can't laugh me off or chase me outta the room, 'cause I got a right to talk to him.

(Pause.)

Now, for the last time, can I see your husband?

FLO: No.

MARILYN: Screw you.

(MARILYN *gathers her purse and heads for the door.*)

FLO: I no longer have a husband. At last, God has seen fit to bless me with a child.

(MARILYN *stops.*)

Every morning, I feed him. I cut his meat into small squares, and I mash his vegetables. At night, I dust him with powder. I hold him when he cries during sleep. That is my purpose now, that is my function. To mother.

MARILYN: You're scaring me.

FLO: Though you are too late to save my husband, perhaps you will save me.

MARILYN: "Save" you?

FLO: Ten hours a day, five days a week, you at his side. Perhaps you know. Perhaps you can tell me.

MARILYN: Anything I got to tell belongs to him, not you.

FLO: Park is no longer the man you knew. One morning I awoke to find him collapsed across his desk, like a marionette whose strings had been cut by some giant, malevolent child. I reached instinctively to close his eyelids. That's when I felt his breath against my palm.

MARILYN: Holy shit.

FLO: Torn paper. Bottles of ink. He had been writing something. And then he had . . . he had been . . . Park had been eating.

MARILYN: He'd been *what?*

FLO: His mouth was a brilliant blue, like some nocturnal clown. He'd been giving birth to pages upon pages of prose, then devouring them. At the hospital, they pumped his stomach. A habit of his, it seems, cannibalizing his own words. The doctors surmised he had been doing it for quite some time. His belly was round and ripe with pulp. Pregnant, if you will.

MARILYN: This is bullshit; you're making this up.

FLO: It was the ink. Trichlorethylene. Highly toxic, even in small doses, and Park, I'm afraid, was prolific.

MARILYN: Three thousand miles I came. You're not scaring me away with half-ass stories.

FLO: Unfortunately, he has lost the capacity for speech. He cannot tell me the content of his manuscript. It obsesses me. What was he compelled to write that was too cancerous to read? I still hunt the carpet for scraps. For fragments from which I can divine meaning. There are a few.

(FLO *crosses over to the desk. She pulls a few paper scraps from beneath a Plexiglas shield.*)

"Bartók . . . A safe-deposit box . . . the poison I inflict in tiny drops."

(*She arranges and rearranges the scraps on the surface of the desk like puzzle pieces.*)

I form quilts in my mind with these words, hoping to find a pattern that renders them explicable and not terrifying. To date, I have one clue.

(FLO *picks up a small lacquered box. She opens it.*)

In the emergency room, they found a tattered piece of stationery still lodged in his mouth. Smudged but not illegible. One word. A name.

(FLO *removes a final scrap of paper. She offers it to* MARILYN.)

"Milo."

(MARILYN *stiffens. Her face turns ashen.*)

Please. Is that a name that you have heard before?

(*The two women stare at each other.*)

MARILYN: I'm sorry.

FLO: An acquaintance at work.

MARILYN: I don't—

FLO: A relative.

MARILYN: I can't—

FLO: The architect of my husband's fate.

MARILYN: I don't know.

FLO: Please. Tell me.

MARILYN: There were no Milos.

FLO: The truth.

MARILYN: Himself. Milo's him.

(*Purposefully,* FLO *crosses over to the bedroom door and opens it. The soft beep and steady pump of life-support machinery. Pale blue light streams into the main room.* FLO *moves aside.* MARILYN *takes several slow steps toward the door. When she peers inside, she gasps and grabs the door frame for support. Lights rise on* PARK. *He lies in a hospital bed. An oxygen tent, a heart monitor. Tubes stream out from under the sheets and rise into the sky in an almost weblike pattern. His face is contorted with pain.*)

FLO: I sit next to him now, his hand limp in mine, for hours. His face has become a sort of mask, a look lodged somewhere between anger and genuine madness. I can't place his expression, and then it comes back to me. A story I once heard, a folktale told by the Burundi in Africa. At the dawn of time, they say, God walked among men, on the earth. God ate with man, slept with man, and toiled with man. With his hands, he molded from clay the children who were born to man. One day God slipped, and formed a crippled baby. Nevertheless, he breathed life into the child, and set it forth into the world, into the waiting arms of a hopeful mother. The father of the child was not happy. He thought the child a cheat, an unkind ruse played by a hapless God. He became unhinged: an anger so great he sharpened a knife and lay in wait, hoping to slaughter his Maker. But God, who saw all things, knew of the plan, and so he fled to the sky for safety. There he sits, in darkness, safe from our pitiful wrath. Man is left alone to rail noiselessly at the sky. I look at my husband, strapped to a white bed, and I see that fury.

(Pause. From offstage a horn blast.)

Park said you have a child. What is the name of your child?

(MARILYN steps away from the bedroom door. She pulls herself together, then turns and stares directly at FLO.)

MARILYN: Once Park came to the hospital, late. He put his hand up under the little tent, and he stroked Milo's cheek. He felt something for our boy. He was a good father.

FLO: Thank you.

(More insistent horn blares.)

MARILYN: I hafta. My home. Dash'll be ripped. One helluva drive. Early start, you know.

(MARILYN's at the front door.)

I gotta life now, see?

(MARILYN *exits.* FLO *stands alone. Outside,* DASH *lays on the horn. Two shafts of light rise; one left, one right. They brighten until they are white-hot.*)

Scene 11

Faraway drums.

FLO *and* YOBO MUNDE *step forward to occupy each pool of light.*

YOBO MUNDE: Tell the woman Baku is alive. Tell the woman he has grown faster than floodwaters. Faster than disease. Tell her he has triumphed over Nature, the force which carved him. Tell her he has the strength of ten men, now in his bones. His feet are deep in the soil. His toes are taking root. His arms are tree branches, strong enough to pluck the sun from its roost, so he might cradle it in his palms. Tell her he will go forth, and he will plant children. In the stifling heat, they will grow. In barren sand, they will grow. Without food, without milk, but with touch, they will grow. Tell the woman that the souls of her un-born children rage like fire in his eyes.

(FLO *stretches out her hand to reach* YOBO. *He, in turn, reaches for her. A beam of light catches their outstretched fingers, yearning for each other, across continents, across seas. From the sky, a trickle of sand. It cascades through their fingers. The drums build. Blackout.*)

Scene 12

FLO, *on her nursery stool, reads from a picture book to her invisible class.*

FLO: "All day long Mr. Hodge-Podge tinkered, making marvelous inventions from broken baubles and throwaway toys. One fine spring day, Mr. Hodge-Podge made a miracle. With two old shoes and a wastebasket, with old bubble gum and a bicycle tire, Mr. Hodge-Podge built a little boy. He had ball bearings for eyes, and soup spoons instead of proper ears."

(FLO closes the book, marking the page with her finger. She admires its cover.)

Such a simple book. This is, I think, my favorite book.

(She opens the book again and continues reading.)

"Mr. Hodge-Podge unzipped the boy's mouth and a butterfly flew willy-nilly into the air. 'His first word!' cried Mr. Hodge-Podge, catching the bug in his hand. 'I'll pin it to the wall, so I will remember it always. . . .' "

(A pause. FLO smiles, lost in thought. Lights slowly fade to black.)

Quills

Fanaticism in me is the product of persecutions I have endured from my tyrants. The longer they continue their vexations, the deeper they root my principles in my heart.

—*The Marquis de Sade in a letter to his wife*

Quills was originally produced by the New York Theatre Workshop (James C. Nicola, artistic director; Nancy Kassak Diekmann, managing director) in New York City on November 3, 1995. It was directed by Howard Shalwitz; the set design was by Neil Patel; the costume design was by James Schuette; the lighting design was by Blake Burba; the sound design was by Darron L. West; and the production stage manager was Kate Broderick. The cast was as follows:

DOCTOR ROYER-COLLARD . . . . Daniel Oreskes

MONSIEUR PROUIX / A LUNATIC . . . . Kirk Jackson

RENÉE PÉLAGIE . . . . Lola Pashalinski

ABBÉ DE COULMIER . . . . Jefferson Mays

THE MARQUIS . . . . Rocco Sisto

MADELEINE LECLERC /
    MADAME ROYER-COLLARD . . . . Katy Wales Selverstone

CHARACTERS

DOCTOR ROYER-COLLARD

> Chief physician at the Charenton Asylum.

MONSIEUR PROUIX

> A celebrated architect.

RENÉE PÉLAGIE

> The grief-stricken wife of a madman.

ABBÉ DE COULMIER

> Administrator at the asylum.

THE MARQUIS

> The asylum's most notorious inmate.

MADELEINE LECLERC

> The seamstress at Charenton; sixteen and quite lovely.

A LUNATIC

> A madman heard through a chink in the wall.

MADAME ROYER-COLLARD

> The doctor's wife, a woman of considerable appetites.

SETTING

The Charenton Asylum: the office of Dr. Royer-Collard, the quarters of the Marquis, and the hospital's charnel house. The year is 1807.

ACT ONE

Scene 1

DR. ROYER-COLLARD, MONSIEUR PROUIX, RENÉE PÉLAGIE.

DR. ROYER-COLLARD: I trust you are discreet, Monsieur Prouix. The delicacy of my situation here requires a candor far greater than I would otherwise employ.

MONSIEUR PROUIX: Have no fear, Doctor. There's room in my grave for your secrets as well as my own.

DR. ROYER-COLLARD: I am the newly appointed chief physician of the Charenton Asylum. It is my solemn duty to restore this ailing institution to its former glory. I hope you won't accuse me of grandiosity if I suggest that Charenton is my France, and I am her Napoleon.

MONSIEUR PROUIX: It's a metaphor both stirring and apt!

DR. ROYER-COLLARD: The Ministry has granted me this post because in their generous estimation I am a staunchly moral man, of impeccable character and iron resolve. My wife, on the other hand, is less stalwart than I.

MONSIEUR PROUIX: Oh, dear.

DR. ROYER-COLLARD: She has a frivolous nature and boundless appetites which render her . . .

MONSIEUR PROUIX: Yes?

DR. ROYER-COLLARD: . . . *prone to inconstancy.*

MONSIEUR PROUIX: So many women are, Doctor! Their constitutions are not so fully evolved as our own. They fall prey to seduction as readily as you or I catch a summer cold.

DR. ROYER-COLLARD: Often I've been tempted to chain her at the heel, or secure a cow bell round her neck, so I'll be kept alert of her whereabouts.

MONSIEUR PROUIX: Many a man has enforced worse measures in the name of fidelity.

DR. ROYER-COLLARD: While I was delighted to accept this post in the provinces, she was loath to leave Paris. I forced her to abandon all she holds most dear. Her art teacher. Her gardener. And a frisky little footman named Hercule.

MONSIEUR PROUIX: But she followed you here to Saint-Maurice nonetheless. Perhaps she favors her husband after all.

DR. ROYER-COLLARD: It was bribery, not steadfastness, which enticed her. I promised her a château to rival Fontainebleau.

MONSIEUR PROUIX: Hence, my employ . . .

DR. ROYER-COLLARD: You must construct a home of such grand design, so full of beauty and diversion, that she is never inclined to leave it.

MONSIEUR PROUIX: I spent all morning, sir, in pursuit of that very end.

DR. ROYER-COLLARD: And?

MONSIEUR PROUIX: I'm afraid your wife is as extravagant as she is charming. When I suggest granite for the foyer, she's quick to counter with Peruvian marble. The tapestries she has prescribed for your boudoir are no less than spun gold, and the dining set she fancies is inlaid with bone carved from the antler of a rare species of elk common only to the Himalayas.

DR. ROYER-COLLARD: So that's the price she extorts for fealty?

MONSIEUR PROUIX: Why, the proposed garden alone could bankrupt a man.

DR. ROYER-COLLARD: Spend what you must.

MONSIEUR PROUIX: With all due respect, sir, your resources are finite.

DR. ROYER-COLLARD: I'm well aware of my own finances.

MONSIEUR PROUIX: Why, even the cost of lumber—

DR. ROYER-COLLARD: Whatever you require, I'll provide!

MONSIEUR PROUIX: Pardon me, Doctor, I meant no insult. . . .

DR. ROYER-COLLARD: More than my marriage is at stake, Monsieur Prouix. If my wife runs rampant here in Saint-Maurice, the Ministry will call my very competence into question. I can hear them now. "We've entrusted over five hundred madmen to his care. How can he keep the lunatics at bay when he can't even harness his own wife?"

MONSIEUR PROUIX: Excuse me for saying it, sir, but I never dreamed a man of your pragmatism and reserve could be so swayed by a woman's influence.

DR. ROYER-COLLARD: She's a rare bird, Monsieur Prouix. I intend to keep her caged.

(From offstage, a woman's voice.)

RENÉE PÉLAGIE (Offstage.): I must see the doctor at once!

DR. ROYER-COLLARD: What the devil—

MONSIEUR PROUIX: Is that the sound of duty calling?

DR. ROYER-COLLARD: It more than calls, monsieur. It screeches.

RENÉE PÉLAGIE (Offstage.): It's beyond urgent! It's dire!

(The door swings open and RENÉE PÉLAGIE storms in, distraught.)

Scene 2

RENÉE PÉLAGIE, DR. ROYER-COLLARD, MONSIEUR PROUIX.

RENÉE PÉLAGIE: I beseech you, Doctor, let me speak!

DR. ROYER-COLLARD: But, madame, I do not even know you. It is customary to write first, requesting an appointment.

RENÉE PÉLAGIE: Desperation has driven me past etiquette headlong into frenzy!

DR. ROYER-COLLARD: My schedule is not subject to the whims of lunatics.

RENÉE PÉLAGIE: I beg to differ, Doctor. You work in a madhouse. Your every waking moment is governed by the insane.

DR. ROYER-COLLARD: Shall I call for the guard and have you removed?

RENÉE PÉLAGIE: You have a choice. Hear me out or watch as I curdle and die before you, a victim of my own cancerous grief. Denied its expression, I will surely be poisoned by it, and collapse at your feet, a spent cipher, a corpse.

(DR. ROYER-COLLARD *turns to* MONSIEUR PROUIX.)

DR. ROYER-COLLARD: Excuse us a moment, won't you, Monsieur Prouix?

MONSIEUR PROUIX: But of course.

(*He withdraws.* DR. ROYER-COLLARD *addresses* RENÉE PÉLAGIE.)

DR. ROYER-COLLARD: I beg you—be succinct.

RENÉE PÉLAGIE: I have fallen prey to yet another abomination in this unending cavalcade of woe which I am doomed to call "my life."

DR. ROYER-COLLARD: And how might I assist you?

RENÉE PÉLAGIE: You are new to Charenton, are you not?

DR. ROYER-COLLARD: I am.

RENÉE PÉLAGIE: Perhaps you are not yet familiar with my husband and his unusual case.

DR. ROYER-COLLARD: He is a patient here, I presume?

RENÉE PÉLAGIE: Quite.

DR. ROYER-COLLARD: His name?

RENÉE PÉLAGIE: I cannot bring myself to say it, Doctor. Its cost has been so dear.

(She hands a calling card to DR. ROYER-COLLARD. *He reacts.)*

DR. ROYER-COLLARD: With all due respect, madame, all France is familiar with your husband.

RENÉE PÉLAGIE: No one knows his reputation better than I, Doctor.

DR. ROYER-COLLARD: I assume that you've come to plead for clemency on his behalf.

RENÉE PÉLAGIE: Oh you do, do you?

DR. ROYER-COLLARD: I'm afraid I can offer nothing more than sympathy. I have the strictest orders, in a writ signed by Napoleon himself, to contain the man indefinitely.

RENÉE PÉLAGIE: It is my dearest hope, Doctor, that he remain entombed forever, that he be deprived of all human contact, and that when at last he perishes in the dank bowels of your institution he be left as carrion for the rodents and the worms.

DR. ROYER-COLLARD: I stand corrected, madame.

RENÉE PÉLAGIE: I have paid in blood, sir, for the mere fact that I am his wife, and he my husband.

DR. ROYER-COLLARD: I see. . . .

RENÉE PÉLAGIE: I don't know which has plagued me more. His grotesque résumé of crimes or their notoriety. When he mutilated that poor beggar, her backside forked through like a pastry shell, no one was more mortified than I. His orgy in the schoolyard—those pitiful children, that lethal pox—well, it rent the fabric of my heart. But I was no less moved when, on a country weekend in Chambéry, our hostess, upon learning I was his spouse, spat a mouthful of Côtes-du-Rhône upon my breast. In that moment, all his cruelties coalesced into the single liquid projectile issuing from her lips.

DR. ROYER-COLLARD: Ironic as it may seem, moral outrage often finds its expression in coarse gesture.

RENÉE PÉLAGIE: Everywhere I go, the same scenario ensues! The other evening, at the opera, I was seated in my box, a few scant meters from the stage. In the midst of her aria, the soprano spotted my face in the crowd. She stopped, midnote. The orchestra ceased its play, and the diva cried, "Look! Here in our midst, *Satan's bride!*" Slowly, a thousand opera glasses turned to stare in my direction. I bolted to the door. Stricken, I hauled myself into the nearest church. There, I pleaded for absolution from my husband's sins. When I left, the very pew in which I sat was yanked from the floor by a trio of priests and carried into the courtyard. There, as they intoned the sacred rite of exorcism, they burned the very wood I had sullied with my behind!

(She dissolves into a spasm of tears.)

Oh, Doctor, forgive my hysteria, but I am a woman plagued!

DR. ROYER-COLLARD: Careful, Marquise! Women who take to screaming in these hallways often land themselves in leg irons.

RENÉE PÉLAGIE: I am no stranger to such contraptions, Doctor.

DR. ROYER-COLLARD: You, too, fell prey to his appetites?

RENÉE PÉLAGIE: It's as though my body were his conscience in cor-
poreal form, scarred beyond all repair.

DR. ROYER-COLLARD: What specifically compelled you to pay this
visit today?

(RENÉE PÉLAGIE *composes herself.*)

RENÉE PÉLAGIE: I dared hope that my husband's incarceration
would allow him to fade from the country's memory. I could
then find freedom in his obscurity. Oh, to take tea again! To be
invited on a garden stroll! To once again know the unfettered
glory of walking down the street without insult. Without
falling debris.

DR. ROYER-COLLARD: I wish it for you, my poor Marquise.

RENÉE PÉLAGIE: But something prevents this happy turn of events.

DR. ROYER-COLLARD: What, exactly?

RENÉE PÉLAGIE: Are you aware, sir, of the charge which precipitated my husband's latest arrest?

DR. ROYER-COLLARD: I am. He authored a scandalous novel. A tale
so pornographic that it drove men to murder, and women to
miscarry.

RENÉE PÉLAGIE: And are you further aware that now, even within
these fortified chambers, his writing continues unchecked?

DR. ROYER-COLLARD: What?

RENÉE PÉLAGIE: Charenton provides a haven most agreeable to his
muse. Endless hours to write without interruption, save for his
meals. Stacks of paper at his disposal, rivers of ink, and always—*always*—a ready quill.

DR. ROYER-COLLARD: I assure you, madame, this is the first I have heard of such goings-on.

RENÉE PÉLAGIE: I thought my husband had been placed here at Charenton, in lieu of prison, so that he could be cured of his corrosive habits.

DR. ROYER-COLLARD: I recognize our failing. I even know its cause.

RENÉE PÉLAGIE: Yes?

DR. ROYER-COLLARD: It pains me to admit that our reputation is one of laxity. A certain Abbé de Coulmier, administrator here, has a constitution more suited to nursing babies than tending the insane. He has removed the wicker dummy, the wire cage, and the straitjacket—tools many consider essential to our trade—and replaced them with musical interludes, watercolor exercises, even Marivaux.

RENÉE PÉLAGIE: I had no idea that art offered salvation from madness. I was of the opinion that most artists are themselves quite deranged.

DR. ROYER-COLLARD: That is the very reason the Ministry has named me to this post. To enforce a more stringent atmosphere.

RENÉE PÉLAGIE: I pray that, for your sake and mine, you succeed at your assigned task.

(A pause. DR. ROYER-COLLARD frowns.)

DR. ROYER-COLLARD: It's not so easily done, madame. We require blacksmiths, to cast new shackles. A battalion of guards. Thumbscrews and pillories, to keep the patients tranquil. I'm afraid our resources are already strained.

RENÉE PÉLAGIE: That is your worry, sir, not mine.

DR. ROYER-COLLARD: On the contrary, madame. If you were to but-
tress your entreaties with, perhaps, the means to oblige them—

RENÉE PÉLAGIE: I am not a wealthy woman.

DR. ROYER-COLLARD: Your husband's legal records routinely cross
this desk. Is it not true that the recent sale of his mansion at La
Coste has granted you a sudden windfall?

RENÉE PÉLAGIE: A trifling nest egg, hardly a fortune.

DR. ROYER-COLLARD: If you are truly determined to step out of the
long, dark shadow of your husband's celebrity—

RENÉE PÉLAGIE: Oh, but I am!

DR. ROYER-COLLARD: Words alone are insufficient.

RENÉE PÉLAGIE: It's beyond perversity. That honor should carry a
price tag!

DR. ROYER-COLLARD: Picture it. A summer's picnic, linens strewn,
an array of succulents, old friends once again deigning to kiss
your hand. "Why, Marquise! Enchanted to see you! Welcome
back from your long, dark descent into the abyss of infamy!"

RENÉE PÉLAGIE: Don't toy with me, Doctor!

DR. ROYER-COLLARD: Now is the time to secure your epitaph.
Renée Pélagie de Montreuil . . . or *"Satan's Bride."*

(A torturous moment for RENÉE PÉLAGIE.*)*

RENÉE PÉLAGIE: Name it and the figure shall be yours.

DR. ROYER-COLLARD: Might I suggest, madame, that we keep our
newfound understanding in confidence.

RENÉE PÉLAGIE: Of course.

DR. ROYER-COLLARD: Far be it from me to press the matter. . . .

RENÉE PÉLAGIE: You may expect my lawyer later this afternoon. I
trust that together you'll arrive at a commensurate sum.

DR. ROYER-COLLARD: I'm eternally in your debt.

RENÉE PÉLAGIE: And I in yours.

(She turns to go, then turns back to DR. ROYER-COLLARD.*)*

Doctor?

DR. ROYER-COLLARD: Marquise?

RENÉE PÉLAGIE: Can I impart to you his cruelest trick?

DR. ROYER-COLLARD: Yes.

RENÉE PÉLAGIE: Once . . . long ago . . . in the folly of youth . . . he made me . . . *love him.*

DR. ROYER-COLLARD: My sympathies, madame.

RENÉE PÉLAGIE: Tell me truthfully. Will my maligned character, stretched so long upon the rack of ignominy, ever regain its natural shape?

DR. ROYER-COLLARD: Take heart!

(He kisses RENÉE PÉLAGIE*'s hand.)*

How suddenly such happiness looms!

Scene 3

DR. ROYER-COLLARD, ABBÉ DE COULMIER, THE MARQUIS.

DR. ROYER-COLLARD: The Ministry informs me that the Marquis falls under your exclusive dominion.

COULMIER: My brethren found him too taxing a patient. A few of the priests were so dispirited they left the order. Father Lely now slaughters pigs in Provence. Father Couvrat is a chimney sweep. And the late Father Buffier is rumored to have buried himself alive rather than minister to the Marquis, in hopes of achieving martyrdom through less rigorous means.

DR. ROYER-COLLARD: And you?

COULMIER: I welcome the challenge.

DR. ROYER-COLLARD: Tell me, what is the Marquis's current regimen?

COULMIER: Ample rest, seclusion, a frigid bath, and twice a week he takes the vapors.

DR. ROYER-COLLARD: He has never once been bled, consigned to the pit, borne the weight of the iron mask?

COULMIER: Forgive my impertinence, Doctor, but you are a learned man, so perhaps you can enlighten me: how can inhumane treatment produce a civilized demeanor? The methods you cite are no less than medieval; I would not visit them upon a dog.

DR. ROYER-COLLARD: And the effect of your preferred prescriptions?

COULMIER: The Marquis no longer roars or spits. He no longer scarifies his skin. His appetite is solid, and his sleep sound.

DR. ROYER-COLLARD: And his prose?

COULMIER: Even a man in the most advanced stages of mental decay is, I believe, still entitled to a modicum of privacy. While I permit him the privilege of his writing exercises, I do not take it upon myself to read them.

DR. ROYER-COLLARD: And yet it seems they might provide the surest barometer of his progress.

COULMIER: Given his newfound docility and reserve, I wouldn't be surprised if his prose, once ripe with the stench of indecency, now borders on the liturgical.

DR. ROYER-COLLARD: A generous supposition.

COULMIER: He is a walking placard for humanitarian strategies in our hospitals, our asylums, even—I'll posit—our Bastilles.

DR. ROYER-COLLARD: Then I'm sure you won't take offense when I tell you that, to affirm his recovery, I requested a thorough search of the Marquis's quarters.

COULMIER: The results, I trust, were unexceptional.

DR. ROYER-COLLARD: Quite the contrary. It yielded some alarming contraband:

(He gestures to the items on his desk.)

Two razors, a purse filled with salt, a wooden prod, newly greased, and a small, iron vise grip of indeterminate usage.

COULMIER: I am no less than stunned, Doctor.

DR. ROYER-COLLARD: These knickknacks are of minimal concern, since they pose no threat to the asylum's general population. However, stashed under a floorboard, we recovered this.

(He pulls a sheaf of papers from his desk.)

A manuscript, some twelve hundred pages long, ready for printing.

COULMIER: Another? So soon?

(DR. ROYER-COLLARD passes the manuscript to COULMIER.)

DR. ROYER-COLLARD: I defy you—in the name of God, France, and all that you hold moral and true—to read it, unmoved.

(COULMIER begins to read it. Lights rise on the opposite side of the stage, revealing THE MARQUIS, seated in his quarters. His hair is elaborately coiffed, and his ruffles are somewhat worn. He writes, quill in hand, reciting as he works.)

THE MARQUIS: Dear Reader, it now falls upon me, your chaperone through the dark waters of the soul, to impart a tale of such mirthless cruelty and moral torpor that I can barely bring my voice above a whisper. So come, perch upon my knee, so you don't miss a word.

(He giggles. COULMIER *glances nervously at* DR. ROYER-COLLARD.*)*

DR. ROYER-COLLARD: Gird yourself. That's mere preamble.

*(*COULMIER *continues to read.)*

THE MARQUIS: On a jutting cliff outside the city of Marseilles, there stood a monastery of most sinister design. To the gullible eye, its windowless facade suggested a simplicity well suited to modest worship. But the true reason for its austerity was far graver: to conceal from the world at large the atrocities occurring within.

(He spins his tale with all the unfettered glee of a mischievous child inventing a lie. He registers delight at each grisly escapade, giddiness at each perversion.)

It was here our young hero first sprang into the world, born of a defrocked priest and a wayward nun. Once the baby was freed from its mother's sin-ripened womb, its parents were duly skewered for their offenses. Bereft and wailing, the child was alone. His only parent was the Church, his only playmates its grim practitioners. Soon he blossomed into boyhood. On his chin, soft down, and between the orbs of his dimpled ass, a blushing rosebud begging to be . . . plucked. Would that he were carrion before vultures! Would that he were a quivering faun trapped in a lion's gaze! *Would that he were anything but a comely boy surrounded by priests!*

COULMIER: I can smell its incipient odor, Doctor.

DR. ROYER-COLLARD: What's that, Abbé?

COULMIÉR: Blasphemy. The last refuge of the failed provocateur.

DR. ROYER-COLLARD: Just wait. He brings new vigor to an old standard.

THE MARQUIS: So great was his beauty, so pungent was his youth, that the black-robed friars had christened him with the name Ganymede. The youth soon became unsurpassed in the field of debauchery. Oh, dear Reader, what evils a man can commit when reason demurs to lust! For these were Ganymede's teachers: an aged monk so withered and limp that frottage was his highest aspiration; an archbishop whose aperture was so fetid and of such slack diameter that it resembled the seat of an untended privy more than any human hole—

(COULMIER *swoons, dabbing at his brow.*)

COULMIER: Look at me; I'm awash in perspiration.

THE MARQUIS: A lapsed prelate who, when Ganymede felt Nature's rustlings, insisted that he use his gaping maw as its receptacle—

COULMIER: Heaven forfend!

THE MARQUIS: And, most atrociously, a Viennese cardinal and his participatory horse.

COULMIER: Participatory?

DR. ROYER-COLLARD: Picture it!

COULMIER: Nature herself was never more abused!

THE MARQUIS: Ganymede weathered these requests with the cool detachment of one already dulled by life's demands. He had no time to pursue the twin luxuries of faith and piety; his only aim was to survive. And to do so he knew he must offer his flesh, naked on a plate, for the frantic lapping of a hundred unholy tongues. This is what a life spent in the bosom of the Church had taught him. . . .

DR. ROYER-COLLARD: Endless pages of philosophy follow.

(COULMIER *begins frantically flipping through the pages.*)

THE MARQUIS: No God—blah, blah, blah—dominion through force—
blah, blah, blah—the inevitability of chaos—blah, blah, blah—

COULMIER: But what of the boy's fate?

DR. ROYER-COLLARD: Swept away by the story, are you?

COULMIER: It's necessary to know his end in order to gauge the full
measure of the Marquis's depravity.

DR. ROYER-COLLARD: Page 73. I've folded the corner.

(COULMIER *regards* DR. ROYER-COLLARD *for a moment.*)

THE MARQUIS: Soon Ganymede was adopted by the Duc de Blangis,
a rank old pedophile with a penchant for gutter trade. "What
soft skin you have!" cooed the Duc when the boy lay exposed
before him. "So womanish! So suitable for lechery! I will not
have it wrinkle or coarsen; rather, I'll preserve its sheen forever!" With that, the Duc uncorked a vial of linseed oil. He
dribbled it over the child's nude body, filling each crevice, each
moist valley, till Ganymede shone like an eel. Then he wrapped
the boy in freshly harvested donkey hide. "Here you'll stay," the
Duc commanded, "until you've absorbed each drop. Only then
will we commence with our debauch!" Accustomed to the most
vile abuses, the boy found such treatment a happy respite. The
hide was warm and soft, and daily the Duc fed him the most astonishing foods. Marzipan, hot sugared pastries, cream-filled
cakes and glacés. "Mon Dieu," sighed the boy, "I could live this
life forever!" Soon, however, Ganymede realized the appalling
truth.

COULMIER: What cruel twist has the Marquis in store?

THE MARQUIS: The calculating Duc had not cured the enveloping hide, and so as the boy's body, gorged with desserts, grew swollen like a great pink bladder its casing began to shrink.

COULMIER: Dear God!

THE MARQUIS: "Please," beseeched the boy. "Split the hide, so I might breathe free!" The Duc merely laughed, and silenced his victim with a few spoonfuls of mousse. The boy could suffocate or swallow, so swallow he did, increasing his girth and thereby increasing his torment. Soon the child was prepared to strike any bargain. "Free me from this leather prison and you can use me as your slave!" "Don't you see, little one?" purred the Duc. "My delectation has already begun." In time, Ganymede's back arched in a circle and his shoulders met. He felt his rib cage close upon itself, like a lady's purse snapped shut at the opera. With that, the Duc de Blangis released his loins, the hot seed of his tumescence spiraling through the air like molten lava from some belching volcano—

COULMIER: Enough!

(THE MARQUIS *shrugs. The lights on him fade.*)

DR. ROYER-COLLARD: That's only the first chapter.

COULMIER: Already he has cataloged every known vice—and some hitherto unknown!

DR. ROYER-COLLARD: And that page is followed by eleven hundred and fifty-seven more.

COULMIER: Astonishing.

DR. ROYER-COLLARD: Imagine if this wound its way among the inmates.

COULMIER: I'd sooner introduce a match to tinder.

DR. ROYER-COLLARD: This man is licentious. *Turpitudinous.*

COULMIER: And *prolific!*

DR. ROYER-COLLARD: And to think, only moments ago you labeled him a triumph of rehabilitation.

COULMIER: I'm driven to distrust my own capacity for judgment.

DR. ROYER-COLLARD: You treat him like a man, Abbé; therein lies your error. In faculties, he's nothing but an errant child. Each time you coddle him, you invite more of his dark mischief. Don't you see? He's all but begging to be strung up by the toes.

COULMIER: It chills me to think, sir, that our institution might perpetuate the very horrors the Marquis himself so painstakingly describes.

DR. ROYER-COLLARD: What is most reassuring to the lunatic? The sight of the shackles, waiting for him. It's like a balm to his uneasy mind; in them, he sees the architecture of all civilization.

COULMIER: I implore you, do not insist that I negate my principles. Let me continue in my charitable course.

DR. ROYER-COLLARD: Understand that his reformation is an urgent priority.

COULMIER: I'll do all that I can.

DR. ROYER-COLLARD: Do more. Otherwise I'll be forced to report to the Ministry that the inmates are indeed running the asylum.

Scene 4

MADELEINE, THE MARQUIS.

MADELEINE: I've darned your stockings, and the hem on your nightdress.

THE MARQUIS: I won't wear them, Madeleine. Never again, my little rosette, my pearl—

MADELEINE: Don't start, you filthy old goat.

THE MARQUIS: I'll enshrine them in my closet, knowing it was your fingers which drove the needle through their membranes!

MADELEINE: Someday I'll use that same needle to sew your mouth shut.

THE MARQUIS: Promises, promises!

MADELEINE: I'm allowed to collect a few extra louis. When it's personal effects I'm repairing.

(THE MARQUIS *gives her some change.*)

THE MARQUIS: Would that these coins purchased your other talents, too!

MADELEINE: That's not all. There's something else I want from you.

THE MARQUIS: You've already stolen my heart, as well as another more prominent organ, south of the equator. . . .

MADELEINE: Mother says I'm not to leave without a story.

THE MARQUIS: A voracious reader, your mother.

MADELEINE: She's stone-blind, on account of all the lye in the laundry kettles. Soaking sheets for lunatics cost the poor lady her sight. I read 'em to her.

THE MARQUIS: Oh?

MADELEINE: Every night at about eight we sit at the table and I start in reciting from wherever it was we left off the night before. Sometimes, when it's a beheading, or some broken thing is locked in a dungeon, crying for the loss of her chastity, my mother's face goes pale, she sets down her glass, and she says—

THE MARQUIS: Yes?

MADELEINE: "Read that part again!"

THE MARQUIS: Nothing like a good tingle, is there, Madeleine?

MADELEINE: Sometimes I have to slam the book shut just to catch my breath. Mama turns all atwitter, cranky for the delay, and makes me forge on.

THE MARQUIS: When the priests taught you to read, did they foresee your taste in novels?

MADELEINE: You're not the only one, mind you. We read Monsieur de Laclos, and Louvet de Couvray. "But when we want a good scare," says Mama, "make it the Marquis!"

THE MARQUIS: Do I frighten you now, Madeleine?

MADELEINE: You? Frighten me? That's a good one! I tell Mama, "If you could only see him you wouldn't tremble so at his tales. Who'd have thought such a spent body could still boast such a fertile mind?"

THE MARQUIS: That's the only frontier I have left, dearest. And what kind of story shall it be tonight?

MADELEINE: Something to make our blood run cold and set our cheeks aflame.

THE MARQUIS: Just how bad would you like it to be?

MADELEINE: Past all redemption, please.

THE MARQUIS: I have just the manuscript, inspired by these very surroundings. The unhappy tale of a virginal nursemaid, the darling of the lower wards, where they entomb the hopelessly deranged.

MADELEINE: Is it awfully violent?

THE MARQUIS: Most assuredly.

MADELEINE: Is it terribly erotic?

THE MARQUIS: Fiendishly so!

MADELEINE: Is it both at once?

THE MARQUIS: But of course!

MADELEINE: Ooh, that sounds like a fine one!

THE MARQUIS: But it comes with a price.

(He holds up the manuscript.)

A kiss for each page.

MADELEINE: My, that's steep.

THE MARQUIS: There are, of course, lesser authors waiting to be read. . . .

MADELEINE: Must I administer the kisses directly or might I blow them?

THE MARQUIS: The price, my coquette, is as firm as my javelin.

MADELEINE: Oh, you! You talk same as you write.

(She sighs, then kisses THE MARQUIS. He gives her a page. She kisses him again. Another page. A third time, a third page.)

It's a long story, this one.

THE MARQUIS: And this, the climax of the story, comes at a higher cost!

MADELEINE: What's that, then?

THE MARQUIS: Sit on my lap.

MADELEINE *(Mutters as she crawls into his lap.)*: You demand a lot from your readers, you do.

THE MARQUIS: Needless to say, the story's thrilling conclusion comes at a premium.

MADELEINE: What would that be, pray tell?

THE MARQUIS *(Whispers in her ear, his tone low and hypnotic.)*: Your maidenhead. And then you must turn your needle and thread upon yourself. Sew it up as tightly as when you were a virgin, and come back to me, renewed, so I can deflower it a second time.

(MADELEINE *stares at him for a moment, stunned. Suddenly she slaps him, hard.*)

MADELEINE: Some things belong on paper, others in life. It's a blessed fool who can't tell the difference.

(COULMIER *appears. He observes* THE MARQUIS *and* MADELEINE, *entangled. He clears his throat.*)

COULMIER: Mademoiselle Leclerc.

MADELEINE: You're in the nick of it, Abbé. This old lech forgot himself for a moment. He thought I was a character in one of his nasty books.

(MADELEINE *thrusts her tongue out at* THE MARQUIS *and exits.*)

Scene 5

COULMIER, THE MARQUIS.

COULMIER: It is those same books which have precipitated my visit, dear Marquis.

(THE MARQUIS *uncorks a decanter.*)

THE MARQUIS: Care for a splash of wine, Abbé?

COULMIER: Here? Now? It's not yet noon.

THE MARQUIS: Conversation, like certain portions of the anatomy, always runs more smoothly when lubricated.

COULMIER: Why, yes, thank you.

(THE MARQUIS *pours two glasses of wine.*)

THE MARQUIS: It's a rare vintage, from an obscure village in Bordeaux. Rather than crush the grape underfoot, they place the fruit on the belly of a bride and reap its juices when the young husband steers his vessel into port.

COULMIER: Oh, my.

THE MARQUIS: Swish it gently in the glass before tasting. You can smell the perfume in her hair, and the beads of sweat from that nether region called love's temple. A full-bodied flavor with just a hint of wantonness?

(COULMIER *stops mid-draught, coughs, and sets his glass down.*)

COULMIER: As you know, most esteemed Marquis, the staff has done its utmost to render you comfortable here.

THE MARQUIS: It's true, dear heart, you've spoiled me pink.

COULMIER: A canopied bed, in lieu of a straw mat. An ample library, including the latest medical volumes, as per your request. A settee of yellow Utrecht velvet, and a portrait of your very own father, painted in miniature upon an ivory horn, and . . . lest we forget . . . a well-stocked supply of paper, with enough quills to feather an ostrich.

THE MARQUIS: For these, I am most grateful.

COULMIER: We are delighted that Charenton so readily invokes your muse.

THE MARQUIS: Stories tumble from me here faster than I can record them.

COULMIER: This has not escaped our attention. Pleased though I may be at your prolificity, I'm afraid I have to place certain censures upon your quill, dear Marquis.

THE MARQUIS: Not content to be my jailer, you're now my editor as well?

COULMIER: From this moment forward, I beseech you, for your own good as well as mine—no more ribald tales!

THE MARQUIS: You didn't care for my little Ganymede.

COULMIER: No.

THE MARQUIS: But you read about his exploits nonetheless.

COULMIER: Yes.

THE MARQUIS: By candlelight you licked the words off the paper and rolled them around in your mouth. You swallowed. You succumbed.

COULMIER: My interest was professional, sir, not prurient.

THE MARQUIS: Did you read every word? Or did you run straight away to the dog-eared pages?

COULMIER: Enough to discern the novel's tenor.

THE MARQUIS: And?

COULMIER: It stirred in me a most pressing desire.

THE MARQUIS: To copulate?

COULMIER: To bathe. It's offensive, in every realm. A compendium of perversities.

THE MARQUIS: Surely if such phenomena exist in nature, then they are fair game in fiction. . . .

COULMIER: You expect me to believe that these atrocities occur?

THE MARQUIS: We don't run in the same circles, do we, my cherub?

COULMIER: I work in a madhouse. Still, I've never seen anything such as you describe.

THE MARQUIS: If they can be dreamt, they can be done.

COULMIER: Permit me, for a moment, to play the role of critic, dear Marquis. Morally, your tale has a smug tone, condemning its principals while delighting in their misbehavior. It purports to advocate virtue by detailing vice. At best, a wobbly proposition.

THE MARQUIS: Why must morality serve as the book's barometer? It's an entertainment, my persimmon, not a moral treatise.

COULMIER: But in a world too often governed by man's fickle tastes, morality is our only bedrock. It is the golden standard against which we are all judged.

THE MARQUIS: But that's preposterous! Morality is a convenience, nothing more!

COULMIER: Surely a man so oft afoul of the law is more cognizant of its boundaries.

THE MARQUIS: There was a time, my love, when I was brought to trial for the depucilating of seven very young girls. Mind you, all I did was spoon them diuretics—the other charges were hysterical. Nevertheless, I was sentenced to the Bastille. The judge blamed my behavior on my noble birth. "You aristocrats," he bellowed, "feasting on the helpless, nourishing your vices on the spoils of the poor! Soon the worm will turn!" *Well!* When the Bastille was stormed and liberated by the mob, they told me I was one of their own! "Impoverished slave," they cried. "Puppet of the ruling class! Let us reward your suffering with freedom!" Who, I implore you, was right? The judge? The mob? One insisted I was a perpetrator; the other, a victim. Each claimed it was a matter of *moral principle*. What in this story is constant? Some abstract morality, applied to the tatters of my tiny life? I think not! *Only me!* Only me and those seven little girls, left to spend eternity evacuating in the loo. . . .

COULMIER: You risk offending more than man; you risk offending God.

THE MARQUIS: Oh, please!

COULMIER: Theologically, your story is utterly damning; Ganymede born of the union between two lapsed celibates. His parents are more Dionysian than Catholic; they make a mockery of their chastity vows.

THE MARQUIS: It's chastity vows that make a mockery of men. My uncle, the Abbé de Sade, was esteemed by his betters in the Church. Yet routinely he kept one trollop in the confessional, one in the sacristy, and one—naked and squealing—under the baptismal font! That way, between each Sunday Mass, there was always a ready sheath for his sword! Once—and this, my adorable Coulmier, turns even my cheeks to a rosy hue—he administered communion with a harlot under his robes! While he poured Christ's blood into its silver chalice and drank, she imbibed a liquid no less divine!

COULMIER: I fear, Marquis, that sacrilege comes as naturally to you in conversation as it does upon the page.

THE MARQUIS: An atheist cannot be sacrilegious. The word does not exist in his vocabulary. Sacrilege is the exclusive province of the devout.

COULMIER: Men like your uncle may fail the Bible, but that hardly merits dismissing its precepts.

THE MARQUIS: But, darling, my novel does not subscribe to the Bible's precepts, and as such it should not be held to them in your critique.

COULMIER: How, then, should I evaluate it? As political allegory, perhaps? All right, then. It's simplistic and panders to popular sentiment. Ganymede as France, born the bastard child of the Church, indulged by the decadent bourgeoisie, gorged with all manner of useless opulence, until at last his own body revolts against him . . .

THE MARQUIS: Where does the novel profess to be a political tract?

COULMIER: What, then, does it desire to be?

THE MARQUIS: Literature, my pet!

COULMIER: Frankly, it even fails as an exercise in craft. Note the tireless repetition of the words "nipple" and "pikestaff."

THE MARQUIS: There I was taxed, it's true.

COULMIER: The narrative itself is little more than an exhaustive list of mayhems—sans character, sans theme. And such puny scope! Where are its heroes? Its virtues and triumphs?

THE MARQUIS: Must we record only those phenomena that ennoble us as creatures? What unites us, my precious? Common language? A universal God? Shared codes of law and conduct? No. These vary from one population to the next. Fads and habits, nothing more! Did you know, heavenly man, that in France a husband with six wives would be executed, while in darkest Borneo that same man would be crowned king?

COULMIER: But surely there are verities which exceed geography!

THE MARQUIS: Yes! Primal desire—that's unchanging! Every man from Paris to China feels the same urgent stirring in his loins.

COULMIER: Lust is our only denominator?

THE MARQUIS: Of course not!

COULMIER: Pray tell, what other constants do you cite?

THE MARQUIS: We eat, we shit, we kill, and we die.

COULMIER: Your selectivity confirms your contrary nature. We are also born, we fall in love, we give birth. May I suggest that you endeavor to write a new novel which embraces those verities?

THE MARQUIS: Man has already deluded himself into believing those illusions underlie his life; why does he need a novel to further them?

COULMIER: Not only would it prove more felicitous to its readers but it might perform a cathartic function upon its author.

THE MARQUIS: How so, my dear?

COULMIER: It might assuage your libertine dementia. Your current prose only aggravates it.

THE MARQUIS: If Mother Nature didn't want me to tickle my own fancy, she would not have provided me with two industrious hands. I write with one, leaving the other palm free to enjoy the fruits of the first.

COULMIER: He who lives in darkness cowers in the light, while he who lives in the sun radiates it. Step into the sun for a while, Marquis.

THE MARQUIS: Permit me to extend your metaphor.

COULMIER: Be my guest.

THE MARQUIS: He who sits in the sun is often blinded by it. Then, vulnerable and incognizant, he is devoured by the forces of darkness. Better to stare the fuckers in the face, yes?

COULMIER: And therein lies the path to happiness?

THE MARQUIS: Therein lies survival.

COULMIER: I hope you won't take offense if I suggest that you reject happiness because you fear it is beyond your reach.

THE MARQUIS: My lamb! My beguiling young fool! You're not the man to counsel me in happiness or its pursuit.

COULMIER: Why not? I am content.

THE MARQUIS: Happiness for you, my little kumquat, is achieved through strict adherence to society's mandates. Most men follow this hackneyed passage. Like eager children set loose on a scavenger hunt, they dart about in search of the assigned baubles—wives, offspring, gainful employ, handsome homes. . . . And when they have accrued them all—voilà! The promised treasure is won—happiness ensues! But, for me, happiness springs from a different course.

COULMIER: Which is?

THE MARQUIS: To slice through social artifice, shatter its false conventions, and become one with Nature's Cimmerian tide, where only the ruthless excel, and where brute force yields its own treasure! Past etiquette, past decency, past morals—that's where happiness lies, like the winking chasm buried deep in the briars of a woman's groin.

COULMIER: It's true, is it not, Marquis, that most of your adult life has been spent in prison?

THE MARQUIS: My past addresses read like a primer on crime. Vincennes, the Madelonettes, Saint-Lazare, and the Bastille . . .

COULMIER: And it was in such a milieu that you first wielded your pen?

THE MARQUIS: Oh, my angel! Hell itself is the crucible in which I forged my craft. From the citadel at Picpus, I could see the gallows. Day after day during the Terror, I watched the endless procession to the chopping block. Heads, like champagne corks, flying. My only music was the sound of grief. Its melody was the wretched crying of widows and orphaned children; its percussion, the steady rhythm of the falling blade; its bass, the thud of the cadavers as they rolled down the bank into the pit below. Blood flowed in rivers beneath my window, Abbé.

COULMIER: Perhaps it's best not to extrapolate man's character from such surroundings.

THE MARQUIS: Where better? There, stripped of all postures, man's true self surges to the fore!

COULMIER: You've left me no choice.

(He pauses, then speaks resolutely.)

I'm afraid I have to confiscate your paper and your quill.

THE MARQUIS: What?

COULMIER: You heard me.

THE MARQUIS: But they're all I have!

COULMIER: We cure the drunkard by seizing his liquor. We cure the glutton by absconding with his meal. We cure the rapist by castration.

THE MARQUIS: I can weather your reviews, but spare me this!

COULMIER: We must assuage these perverse fantasies.

THE MARQUIS: But don't you agree that my only salvation is to vent them on paper?

COULMIER: Have you considered reading to pass the hours? A writer who produces more than he reads—the sure mark of an amateur.

THE MARQUIS: My writing is involuntary, like the beating of my heart! My constant erection! I can't help it!

COULMIER: Then we shall stop it for you.

THE MARQUIS: Why? Because I don't cater to the moment's tastes?

COULMIER: Because your novels are a symptom of your insanity.

THE MARQUIS: On the contrary, they keep me sane!

COULMIER: I am sorry. Truly.

THE MARQUIS: I'll write dainty stories, then! Odes to virtue!

COULMIER: I'll have Valcour collect the items in question.

THE MARQUIS: What of my faithful readers?

COULMIER: You've written enough for one lifetime.

THE MARQUIS: What of the little seamstress?

COULMIER: She'd do well to steer clear of your influence.

THE MARQUIS: I have a proposition!

COULMIER: You always do.

THE MARQUIS: She's a luscious morsel, Madeleine. What pulsates beneath those skirts is worth succor! I'm certain I could convince her of the benefits inherent in granting favors to a superior. . . .

COULMIER: I don't know who you insult more: her or me.

THE MARQUIS: Then bugger me!

COULMIER: Don't make me ill.

THE MARQUIS: You can plunder every pore, and lob my knob besides! Anything!

COULMIER: Good day, monsieur.

(*He heads for the door.* THE MARQUIS *drops his desperate pose and coos.*)

THE MARQUIS: Oh, Cupid. My little minx . . .

COULMIER: Yes?

THE MARQUIS: Where there's a will, there's a way. And a maniac is matchless for invention.

Scene 6

DR. ROYER-COLLARD, MONSIEUR PROUIX, COULMIER.

DR. ROYER-COLLARD: Ah! Monsieur Prouix! And how is my new house faring?

MONSIEUR PROUIX: I've come to thank you for loosening your purse strings. The rather dramatic increase in funds behooves us both.

DR. ROYER-COLLARD: It better. I've been forced to devise the most creative financing imaginable. . . .

MONSIEUR PROUIX: Your château shall undoubtedly be my master-work!

DR. ROYER-COLLARD: Yours is an enviable profession, Monsieur Prouix.

MONSIEUR PROUIX: Mine, sir?

DR. ROYER-COLLARD: Yes, indeed. You fabricate the design—each plank, each joist, each pilaster—but you leave the execution to others. Your own grand plan is put into action . . . and you never hoist a stone or drive a nail. That's the true measure of a man's authority, isn't it?

MONSIEUR PROUIX: Well, sir. When you put it that way—

DR. ROYER-COLLARD: Is my wife pleased with your progress?

MONSIEUR PROUIX: Yesterday the silk brocade arrived for the walls of her toilette. She was in the throes of delight. Did you know, sir, that her eyes match its color? I flatter myself that the château shall be a tribute to her beauty. Its golden cornices, the hue of her hair. Its alabaster stone, the tint of her bosom.

Its portals, spread ever wide, as frank and inviting as her very nature . . .

(COULMIER *enters.*)

COULMIER: Pardon me, Doctor, but I was summoned at your behest.

DR. ROYER-COLLARD: Yes, of course. Monsieur Prouix. You'll have to complete your little rhapsody another time.

MONSIEUR PROUIX: Happily, sir. Your servant, sir.

(MONSIEUR PROUIX *backs out of the room, bowing.*)

Scene 7

COULMIER, DR. ROYER-COLLARD, MADELEINE, THE MARQUIS.

COULMIER: I'm sorry to interrupt, Doctor, but your missive had an urgent tone.

DR. ROYER-COLLARD: A curious phenomenon has beset Charenton. It seems that the bed sheets, curtains, and towels—usually so pristine—have acquired of late a burgundy tincture. Some of the patients find this most distressing. Accustomed to more sterile hues, they now find themselves bathed in scarlet. It unsettles them.

COULMIER: Surely it's the fault of the laundress, Madame Leclerc. She's quite blind; perhaps her kettles are stained with rust.

DR. ROYER-COLLARD: Our little mystery has a more engrossing denouement. I spoke this morning with Madame Leclerc's daughter, Madeleine.

(*Lights rise on* MADELEINE.)

MADELEINE: I swear I don't know, sir. But it's rather a lovely shade, if I do say so.

DR. ROYER-COLLARD: You realize, of course, that this casts aspersions upon your mother's skills. After all . . . a blind laundress. Would you hire a crippled dancer, or a pianist without hands?

MADELEINE: She's a devoted woman who, in spite of the afflictions it's caused her, stays by her job.

DR. ROYER-COLLARD: You're a spirited girl, aren't you, Madeleine? You would defend your mother to the core?

MADELEINE: I would, sir.

DR. ROYER-COLLARD: And you realize, of course, that to withhold any pertinent information regarding her laxity could cost you both your tenure here?

MADELEINE: You'd sack us, then?

DR. ROYER-COLLARD: Precisely.

MADELEINE: Please, sir! Cast me out upon the street and I'd survive. But my poor mother! Without her sight, and hardly a tooth in her head, she'd soon be dead. And who's to pay for burial? At least here we're guaranteed a pit alongside the morons.

DR. ROYER-COLLARD: Now . . . fully apprised of the situation . . . would you care to amend your earlier statement?

(MADELEINE *pauses. For an excruciating moment, she weighs her options. Then, a resolute answer.*)

MADELEINE: No, monsieur.

DR. ROYER-COLLARD: You are certain.

MADELEINE: I am.

DR. ROYER-COLLARD: Very well. You and yours are to vacate the premises no later than—

MADELEINE: But, monsieur—

DR. ROYER-COLLARD: —no later than noon, at which time—

MADELEINE: It was the Marquis!

DR. ROYER-COLLARD: The Marquis?

MADELEINE: Relieved of paper and pen, but not of the urge to write, he took to his linens!

DR. ROYER-COLLARD: What?

MADELEINE: He wrote his stories on the bed sheets, penning them with the wine from his evening meal. His words bled into the fibers of the cloth.

DR. ROYER-COLLARD: And the nature of these bedtime tales?

MADELEINE: Silly froth, mostly.

DR. ROYER-COLLARD: Can you be more explicit?

MADELEINE: Than the Marquis? Never!

DR. ROYER-COLLARD: If ever there was a time to humor me, Miss Leclerc, it is now.

MADELEINE: It was a preposterous story. So extreme, sir, one can't take it as truth. One can only laugh.

(Lights rise on THE MARQUIS. *He writes on sheets of torn linen, using a stick as a pen, dipping it into his carafe of wine.)*

THE MARQUIS: Here follow the adventures of Monsieur Dolmance, who could not raise his scepter without first submerging it in a vial filled with the tears of maligned virgins. To procure the precious fluid, he first sent his coachmen into the night to kidnap the unsuspecting damsels. A simple line always sufficed: "Mademoiselle, your mother is perilously ill! I must take you to her at once!" Once the maids were sequestered in his dungeon, Dolmance employed many exotic means to harvest their sobs—

wrapping their feet with nettles, salting their wounds, and strafing their backs with his cane. Soon the chalice was filled. Dolmance dunked his harpoon, then lanced each of his wailing captives in turn.

(Lights fade on THE MARQUIS.*)*

DR. ROYER-COLLARD: His scribbling is no less potent for its form!

MADELEINE: After reading them, Mama and I, fearful of their discovery, attempted to wash away the words! And so the vats were polluted!

DR. ROYER-COLLARD: Why would a demure young girl such as yourself, not to mention your aging mother, indulge in such pornography?

MADELEINE: It's hard day's wages, sir, slaving away at the behest of madmen. What we've seen in life, it takes a lot to hold our interest.

DR. ROYER-COLLARD: But why would you want to heap such ghastly fantasies atop an already ghastly existence?

MADELEINE: We put ourselves in his stories, sir. We play the parts. Poor blind Mama, a countess. Me, a courtesan. We've acted them all, you see, regardless of sex—each atheist, each barbarian. And in our dreams, sir . . . it's us doing the killings.

DR. ROYER-COLLARD: *You?*

MADELEINE: Revenge our only motive; rage our only master.

DR. ROYER-COLLARD: To what end?

MADELEINE: If we weren't such bad women on the page, Doctor, I'll hazard we couldn't be such good women in life.

(Lights fade on MADELEINE.*)*

COULMIER: He is indeed a maniac, and matchless at that!

DR. ROYER-COLLARD: You assured me that his writing had ceased.

COULMIER: I hoped it had.

DR. ROYER-COLLARD: The time has come to adopt more punitive means.

COULMIER: If only I trusted their efficacy!

DR. ROYER-COLLARD: When a child pilfers from the candy dish, what do we offer for his reformation? Do we remove temptation altogether, depriving him *and ourselves* of sweetmeats?

COULMIER: No, sir.

DR. ROYER-COLLARD: Do we numb him with philosophy? Great diatribes wherein we debate the nature of good and evil?

COULMIER: I suppose not, sir.

DR. ROYER-COLLARD: Do we promise him an everlasting afterlife, plucking harps, should he return the bonbon to its rightful seat? *Or do we toss him over our knee, yank down his breeches, and thrash him with the rod?*

COULMIER: The latter, unfortunately. And so he learns to fear punishment, rather than to pursue virtue for its own reward.

DR. ROYER-COLLARD: You're a sentimental man.

COULMIER: A practical man, sir. Given the Marquis's unusual tastes, a sound thrashing on bare flesh may not qualify as a "deterrent."

DR. ROYER-COLLARD: I will not be embarrassed a second time.

Scene 8

THE MARQUIS, COULMIER.

THE MARQUIS: My lilac, my dove!

COULMIER: I am not here for sport.

THE MARQUIS: You've come to continue our debate?

COULMIER: Hardly. From now on, you will sleep on a bare mattress.

THE MARQUIS: What, and freeze to death?

COULMIER: And, for good measure, we'll seize the curtains, the towels, and the rugs.

THE MARQUIS: My room, stripped bare?

COULMIER: And nothing but water at every meal.

THE MARQUIS: No, you can't! Deny me anything but the grape!

COULMIER: I am sorry. It's decided.

THE MARQUIS: My circulation—I am not a young man! And my insomnia—alcohol is my only elixir!

COULMIER: Please. That's quite enough.

THE MARQUIS: One drop nightly, that's all I ask! Show mercy, please!

COULMIER: Your meat shall be deboned. You'll have nothing you might fashion as a quill.

THE MARQUIS: Why this sudden torture?

COULMIER: I have not been emphatic enough with you, Marquis. Your degrading habits continue, unabated.

THE MARQUIS: It was only for her.

COULMIER: For whom?

THE MARQUIS: The girl. To entice her back to me. Those splendid afternoons when for a brief, shining moment she toppled these stone walls and set me free.

COULMIER: Her visits, too, will be curtailed.

THE MARQUIS: Her gentle sway may be the final lifeline cast to me. Let me seize it, so I might at last be towed into the warm, cerulean waters of a virtuous life!

COULMIER: The purplest prose is always the least sincere.

THE MARQUIS: It's a potent aphrodisiac, isn't it, my dumpling?

COULMIER: What's that?

THE MARQUIS: Power over another man.

COULMIER: It pains me to censure you. It is not my nature. I am, as you know, a charitable man.

THE MARQUIS: Most.

COULMIER: You're lucky it falls to me to reprimand you. If it were up to the doctor you'd be more than castigated. You'd be flayed alive!

THE MARQUIS: A man after my own heart!

COULMIER: He'd not share your wine, laugh at your vulgarities, and humor you with argument.

THE MARQUIS: You're his sycophant, aren't you? He cracks the whip and you dance. Don't be shy, Coulmier. Jig for me.

COULMIER: Why, you scornful little weasel—

THE MARQUIS: Follow the steps he's taught you; you'd best not improvise. . . .

COULMIER: The doctor and I have our differences, but on this point we uniformly agree: you are a baneful miasma, and you must be purged!

(The MARQUIS begins to dance.)

THE MARQUIS: A one and a two and a three and a four, a one and a two and a three and a four . . .

COULMIER: Good day, Marquis.

(He turns to leave. The MARQUIS stops dancing and hisses.)

THE MARQUIS: Psst. Plug tail. My little skin flute . . .

COULMIER: What now?

THE MARQUIS: In conditions of adversity, the artist thrives.

Scene 9

DR. ROYER-COLLARD, MADELEINE, COULMIER, THE MARQUIS.

MADELEINE *cowers in the office of* DR. ROYER-COLLARD. *He slaps a switch across the surface of his desk.*

DR. ROYER-COLLARD: If your mother lacks either the means or the intelligence to punish you for your foolishness, then perhaps it's my duty to parent you in her stead.

MADELEINE: No, sir! Please, sir!

DR. ROYER-COLLARD: I've no compunction, young lady, about driving my point home with a few swift strokes of the birch.

(COULMIER enters.)

MADELEINE: Dear, Abbé! You're a man of God, sir. Show me one small drop of his infinite mercy. . . .

COULMIER: What's this, child? Shivering like a leaf? Surely you've done no wrong.

MADELEINE: He means to whip me senseless!

COULMIER: Is it true, Doctor?

DR. ROYER-COLLARD: It all depends, Abbé, on her cooperation.

MADELEINE: I've such pale, thin skin! I bruise quickly, and in the most repellent hues!

COULMIER: Shh, child. Gather your wits. I'll see that you come to no harm.

MADELEINE: It's true what the lunatics say, Abbé. You are the kinder man.

COULMIER: Pray, Doctor. What's happened here? And why is this poor girl undone?

DR. ROYER-COLLARD: This morning I sent Valcour to the laundry. I thought, given the recent turn of events, it would be prudent to conduct a search.

COULMIER: And just what did Valcour find there?

MADELEINE: A little gift, that's all, meant only for me.

DR. ROYER-COLLARD: And from whom was this gift bequeathed to you?

MADELEINE: From himself. The Marquis.

COULMIER: The Marquis?

MADELEINE: He pretended to leave some mending for me, outside the door. A souvenir, of sorts.

DR. ROYER-COLLARD: And what was the nature of this memento?

MADELEINE: 'Twas a chapter! Culled from his latest masterpiece!

COULMIER: But that's not possible. His cell is barren. No pen, no paper. His linens stripped, his carafe dry. He has nothing to fashion into pages.

DR. ROYER-COLLARD: That's what you think.

MADELEINE: Some men aren't mad at all. We only think them so, because their genius so far exceeds our own.

DR. ROYER-COLLARD: Show him. *Now!*

(Hesitantly, MADELEINE produces a shirt with broad sleeves and a host of ruffles. It's decorated with cursive.)

COULMIER: Where in God's name did he procure ink?

MADELEINE: Nowhere. He pricked the tips of his fingers with a carving knife. His latest fancies—they're scripted in blood.

COULMIER: Dear God, preserve us.

DR. ROYER-COLLARD: I decided to confront the Marquis myself. When I hoisted open the gates of the South Wing, there he was, strolling about the corridor. His blouse and breeches were covered in script. He'd turned his very wardrobe into text! The idiot Giton was reading his leggings, while the hysteric Michete perused his vest.

(Lights rise on THE MARQUIS. His clothes are awash with words.)

THE MARQUIS: My newest book begins at my right cuff, continues across my back, and completes itself at the base of my left shoe.

COULMIER: Never was a wardrobe more vulgar in design!

THE MARQUIS: Monsieur Bouloir was a man whose sexual appetites might discreetly be described as "postmortem." A habitué of cemeteries, his proudest conquest was that of a maid six decades his senior, deceased a dozen years. The vigor with which he frigged caused her bones to dislodge. Still, he granted her the highest compliment he accorded any woman: *"Well worth the dig!"*

COULMIER: *NOOOOOOOO!*

Scene 10

COULMIER, THE MARQUIS.

COULMIER: You! *You!* Such brazen defiance! Flouncing about like some demented peacock!

THE MARQUIS: Don't tell me. You've come to read my trousers. You'll note the longest sentence trails down the inseam.

COULMIER: How could you! Parading your decadence before the helpless and the sick!

THE MARQUIS: Piffle!

COULMIER: Your stories so aroused poor Michete, we've had to tie him to his bedposts.

THE MARQUIS: Lucky Michete. You tell him that there are some very reputable individuals, notable in French society, who pay good money to be tied to their bedposts.

COULMIER: What am I to do with you, Marquis? The more I forbid, the more you are provoked.

THE MARQUIS: My darling Coulmier. Here, in my dank quarters, I've had ample time to ruminate on our little tussle. And I've come to a conclusion you'll no doubt find deliriously satisfying.

COULMIER: I'm holding my breath.

THE MARQUIS: Headstrong though I may be, I could be convinced to abandon my writing. Quite voluntarily.

COULMIER: And what in God's name would that require? A thousand livres?

THE MARQUIS: Tsk, tsk, tsk. Much cheaper.

COULMIER: Your room, restored to its luster.

THE MARQUIS: Much simpler.

COULMIER: Your freedom.

THE MARQUIS: I wouldn't dream of it.

COULMIER: What, then?

THE MARQUIS: A night, sugarplum, spent with the partner of my choice.

COULMIER: Aha! I should've known!

THE MARQUIS: A lover who will set all pride aside and allow me to plumb with my lubricious engine the twin cheeks of delight.

COULMIER: Write countless unseemly tomes, Marquis. I will not pimp poor Madeleine!

THE MARQUIS: I wasn't talking about Madeleine.

COULMIER: Then who?

THE MARQUIS: *You, my precious.*

(COULMIER *turns a fiery red. He bellows.*)

COULMIER: Off with your clothes!

THE MARQUIS: Coulmier, you rascal!

COULMIER: Off, I say!

THE MARQUIS: Has my proposal so inflamed you?

COULMIER: I do not mean to *flirt*, Marquis!

THE MARQUIS: Oh, but you must, my pumpkin! Sex without flirtation is merely rape!

COULMIER: Damn you, Marquis! You are beyond villainy! You are the Devil! Now strip!

(THE MARQUIS *begins to undress.*)

THE MARQUIS: My doublet?

COULMIER: Off!

THE MARQUIS: My collar?

COULMIER: Off!

THE MARQUIS: My shoes—they're naught but punctuation. . . .

COULMIER: Off!

THE MARQUIS: My chintz, my lace, my gabardine?

COULMIER: Off, off, off!

THE MARQUIS: Permit me to retain my gauzy underpinnings!

COULMIER: Every stitch!

THE MARQUIS: Won't you join me, pony boy?

COULMIER: You shall no longer leave your cell, understood? You'll lay your eyes on none but me from now on!

THE MARQUIS: Such abuse!

COULMIER: You will not render me a fool!

THE MARQUIS: I need not render you a fool!

COULMIER: I have been far too lax with you, monsieur! Now you shall live as our Father intended—less like a man and more like the beast you are! Naked, in a hollow pit!

THE MARQUIS: As lived the noble savages of Lascaux, where even today their glorious paintings remain, undimmed by time!

COULMIER: How dare you defend yourself in art's name! How dare you rank yourself with the likes of Voltaire, Pascal, and Racine!

Their quills are guided by the hand of God, while your every ut-
terance is malignancy unmasked!

(THE MARQUIS *has stripped himself bare, save for his hair.*)

Your wig! Remove your wig!

(THE MARQUIS *does.*)

THE MARQUIS: How prudent you are, Abbé. I'd planned to curl my
locks in the shape of letters and write a paean to buggery that
would trail down my backside and bob at my ass.

COULMIER: You will not spread your insidious gospel, where
tyranny is the norm, and goodness the last refuge of the weak!
Where indifferent Nature rails, untempered by the presence of
God! Where art's magnitude is the breadth of its depravity! No!

THE MARQUIS: No?

COULMIER: You will not even write your own ignominious name!

THE MARQUIS: Tsk, tsk, tsk. Are your convictions so fragile that
mine cannot stand in opposition to them? Is your God so illu-
sory that the presence of my Devil reveals his insufficiency? Oh,
for shame!

COULMIER: May you spend eternity in the company of your
beloved Antichrist, turning on his spit!

(*He makes for the door.*)

THE MARQUIS: My suckling . . . my lip leech . . .

COULMIER: What?

THE MARQUIS: My truest quill lies betwixt my thighs. When it fills
with ink and rises to the fore . . . Oh, the wondrous books it will
write!

Scene 11

THE MARQUIS, MADELEINE.

THE MARQUIS: Madeleine!

MADELEINE: Marquis! Your every inch, exposed!

THE MARQUIS: This is how your employer chooses to keep me. Like a Roman sculpture, undraped!

MADELEINE: I'm ashamed to look!

THE MARQUIS: Surely you've seen a man naked?

MADELEINE: No, sir. It's only been described to me, in your books.

THE MARQUIS: Then you've had a most painstaking teacher. I've devoted many a page to the male form. Its rippling hillsides, its undulating prairies, and its crested mount . . .

MADELEINE: Is your body, then, somewhat . . . representative?

THE MARQUIS: For a man my age, and victim of my calumnies.

MADELEINE: I must say, sir, in your novels you stoke the most unrealistic expectations.

(THE MARQUIS *crosses his legs.*)

THE MARQUIS: You're far crueler than I, my sweet.

MADELEINE: I risk terrible danger, coming to see you this way.

THE MARQUIS: Your life, and your mother's besides.

MADELEINE: It was guilt which ushered me here, stronger than any commandment. How you must hate me.

THE MARQUIS: Never!

MADELEINE: But surely you know it's I who betrayed you to Dr. Royer-Collard. I gave him your soiled bed sheets, and your shirt besides. . . .

THE MARQUIS: And I love you the more for it.

MADELEINE: How can that be?

THE MARQUIS: I may be a scamp, a chancre, and a blight, my blessed Madeleine, but I am not a hypocrite! Don't you see that by informing against me you affirm my principles?

MADELEINE: I'm afraid I don't understand.

THE MARQUIS: You were willing to sacrifice me on the block to achieve your own gain. . . .

MADELEINE: Hence my sorrow!

THE MARQUIS: In the animal kingdom, does the tiger spare his sister the doe? Not when he's hungry! That, Madeleine, is the natural order! A carefully orchestrated cycle of consumption which we all too often violate with our false codes of law and morality. But you! You rose above such petty constructs and fed yourself upon my very carcass.

MADELEINE: And so I am endeared to you?

THE MARQUIS: I stand before you not in rage but in awe.

MADELEINE: You're a queer one, all right.

THE MARQUIS: Can you smuggle a paper and quill to me?

MADELEINE: If only! Mother and I, we're weak with boredom, our evenings spent in silence. For a while, I smuggled home old newspapers from the scullery and read their accounts of the Terror. She found those too barbaric and pined for your stories instead.

THE MARQUIS: Never fear, my angel. I have a plan.

MADELEINE: Let me be its agent, I beg you, as penance for my wrongs against you!

THE MARQUIS: Take note, beloved, of this chink in the stone. I'll whisper a new tale to my neighbor, the lunatic Cleante. He'll in turn whisper it to his neighbor, Dauphin. Dauphin will impart the tale to the retard Franval, and he will impart it likewise to the noisome Bouchon—

MADELEINE: Whose cell lies next to the linen cabinet!

THE MARQUIS: Precisely!

MADELEINE: And there, armed with a quill of my own, I'll receive your story through the wall and commit it to paper!

THE MARQUIS: Voilà!

MADELEINE: Oh, Marquis! How ingenious you are!

THE MARQUIS: Imagine! My scandalous stories whipping through the halls of this mausoleum like some mysterious breeze! A string of tongues, all wagging in service of my prose.

MADELEINE: But with men whose minds are so weak, will your art survive such a journey?

THE MARQUIS: My heinous vision, filtered through the minds of the insane. Who knows? They might improve it!

MADELEINE: I'll practice my hand, Marquis, and do your words justice.

THE MARQUIS: You can take them home to Mother, and on to my publisher besides!

MADELEINE: Only one thing troubles me.

THE MARQUIS: Fear of discovery?

MADELEINE: No. Fear of the inmate Bouchon, the agent closest to me in the line.

THE MARQUIS: Why him, more than any other?

MADELEINE: He holds a torch for me. Once, when I was darning his stockings, he pressed me hard against the wall, and his stinking breath caused my eyes to run. It was the Abbé de Coulmier who saved me.

THE MARQUIS: What of it?

MADELEINE: Well, sir, given the potency of your stories, and the fragility of his brain . . . it might cause a combustion, that's all.

THE MARQUIS: What are we to do, dearest? Shuffle the patients in their cells? That's not within our power. Now, accept the danger or withdraw.

MADELEINE: I accept.

THE MARQUIS: Madeleine?

MADELEINE: Yes, Marquis?

THE MARQUIS: A kiss per page. The price holds.

MADELEINE: But how can I? We're forbidden to meet.

THE MARQUIS: Which is why this time, my pussy willow, I must request payment in advance.

MADELEINE: You're a caution, you are!

THE MARQUIS: Quickly, before we are discovered!

(They consume each other with kisses.)

Scene 12

THE MARQUIS, A LUNATIC, THE VOICES OF THE INSANE.

A crack of thunder. Rain begins to pelt the stone walls of Charenton.

Alone, THE MARQUIS *whispers into a crack in the wall.*

THE MARQUIS: Psst . . . Cleante? Are you there?

(*A voice answers.*)

A LUNATIC: Marquis? Is that you?

THE MARQUIS: Who else would it be?

A LUNATIC: I've the most wonderful news, Marquis! I'm no longer a man! This morning I awoke a bird!

THE MARQUIS: *Quiet!*

A LUNATIC: Tonight I'll fly through the bars of my cell to freedom!

THE MARQUIS: Listen to what I say and report it posthaste to your neighbor Dauphin.

A LUNATIC: I've huge, flapping wings, and a beak for scavenging! And I can warble, too!

(*The* LUNATIC *begins to trill.*)

THE MARQUIS: Cleante!

A LUNATIC: Eh?

THE MARQUIS: I've news for you too, pigeon. This morning I awoke a cat.

A LUNATIC: A cat, Count?

THE MARQUIS (*Dryly.*): Meow.

A LUNATIC: No! I implore you! Anything but that!

THE MARQUIS: If you don't do what I tell you, I'll claw through this wall and eat you alive. I'll sink my little fangs into your drumsticks and suck the marrow straight out of your bones.

A LUNATIC: At your service, Count!

THE MARQUIS: And so we begin. Our story concerns the young heroine Fanchon, a harlot in a harem reputed to be the most varied in all Europe. There, you could plow a Prussian princess, sodomize twins, or tickle the loins of a Hungarian dwarf.

(Down the corridor, faintly, we hear other voices pick up the tale.)

THE VOICES OF THE INSANE: Tickle the loins of a Hungarian dwarf . . . tickle the loins . . . the loins . . . the loins . . . the loins . . .

THE MARQUIS: One day Fanchon was visited by a certain Monsieur De Curval, an accomplished surgeon and an even more re-nowned libertine. He had been barred from many of the city's finer brothels, so lethal were his exploits.

THE VOICES OF THE INSANE: So lethal were his exploits . . . so lethal . . . so lethal . . . lethal . . .

THE MARQUIS: Once they were secluded in her bedchamber, he bade Fanchon strip, and strip she did, with the speed of one un-accustomed to clothing's confinement. As she stood naked be-fore him, he ran his fingers across her skin, pulling apart folds of flesh, inspecting follicles.

THE VOICES OF THE INSANE: Pulling apart folds of flesh . . . folds of flesh . . . flesh . . . flesh . . .

THE MARQUIS: "What shall I ready, Monsieur?" asked Fanchon. "My mouth, my rounded ass, or my Venus mound, my succulent oyster?"

THE VOICES OF THE INSANE: My Venus mound, my succulent oys-ter . . . succulent oyster . . . oyster . . . oyster . . .

THE MARQUIS: "None!" cried Monsieur De Curval, brandishing a scalpel he had hidden in his breast. "With my blade, I'll create new orifices where there were none before! Once hewn, I can thrust my turgid member into regions unsullied by your previ-ous suitors!"

THE VOICES OF THE INSANE: Unsullied suitors . . . suitors . . . suitors . . . suitors . . .

THE MARQUIS: With that, Fanchon expelled a scream so extravagantly pitched that the libertine was obliged to tear out her tongue, cauterizing the wound with a poker from the fire. Next, he splayed her body across the mattress, and with the edge of his knife—

(From offstage, in the distance, a sudden scream. It slices through the air and echoes down the corridor. THE MARQUIS *stops short. His face goes white. He recognizes the howling voice. A bolt of lightning, as powerful as the zap that martyred poor Justine. We see—for a single, blistering moment—the body of* MADELEINE. *She's been hoisted from a rafter in the laundry room, and spins wildly. Her body is a study in carnage. The face of* THE MARQUIS *contorts with pain. A sudden lurch and he collapses on the floor, his body racked by sobs. Blackness. The blowing of the wind. The curtain falls.)*

ACT TWO

Scene 1

RENÉE PÉLAGIE, DR. ROYER-COLLARD.

RENÉE PÉLAGIE: 'Twas a night fraught with terror! I'll never again tremble at tales of the Last Judgment or wince at depictions of the Tortures of the Damned. For hell has indeed been visited upon the earth, and it happened right here at the Charenton Asylum.

DR. ROYER-COLLARD: You overstate our misadventure, madame.

RENÉE PÉLAGIE: Do I? Or are you perhaps reluctant to confront the facts?

DR. ROYER-COLLARD: It was a skirmish, nothing more.

RENÉE PÉLAGIE: Your charge here is to bring order to an unruly hospital. And instead—*on your watch*—the patients revolt, setting their cots ablaze and hurling furniture from their cells. I myself saw a porcelain commode flung from the parapet! And what were the guards doing, I ask you? Stifling the fray? Ha! *They were running for their very lives!*

DR. ROYER-COLLARD: I hasten to assure you—just as I assured the Ministry and the police inspector before you—that harmony within our walls has been restored.

RENÉE PÉLAGIE: All Saint-Maurice turned out for the fracas. Your riot, sir, was the most scrupulously attended social affair since Madame Rougemont's summer cotillion! The Baron de Cordier stood peering through the iron gates in hopes of catching a glimpse of the furor within. Madame Bougival bid her coachmen stop, and scrambled for her telescope. And what did they see? Oh, Doctor, sights so depraved and bizarre that I can barely find the words to describe them!

DR. ROYER-COLLARD: I have a sinking feeling you'll rise to the occasion.

RENÉE PÉLAGIE: Crazed women hiking their skirts to the heavens and pawing at their own femininity! Men with vacant eyes and frothy mouths, their trousers about their ankles, swinging their attributes like pendulums! And who, sir, was the conductor of this demonic orchestra? The ring master of this Luciferian circus? Who? *My husband, of course!*

DR. ROYER-COLLARD: It seems he treated the patients to . . . an oral recitation. They were, regrettably, . . . *overstimulated* . . . by its contents.

RENÉE PÉLAGIE: "Overstimulated," Doctor? They were hanging out the windows, polluting themselves! Charenton became a bawdy house! A brothel for the feebleminded! A cathouse for the loons!

(She collapses into a chair, fanning herself wildly.)

Ah! Ah! He's done it. The Marquis has at long last broken my heart. I can feel it in my breast, cleft in twain. I must have smelling salts! A glass of water! Absinthe! Anything, Doctor, quickly!

(DR. ROYER-COLLARD hands RENÉE PÉLAGIE a small snuff box. She imbibes.)

DR. ROYER-COLLARD: Sparingly, madame. You'll singe your membranes.

RENÉE PÉLAGIE: His little fable traveled far. One of your wards told the cook; the cook told his wife; she told the cobbler; and so on and so on, ad infinitum! Even now, the story is lumbering toward Paris, like some carnivorous, humpbacked beast. Who knows what lascivious behavior it leaves in its wake?

DR. ROYER-COLLARD: My chief worry is not for Charenton or for France but for you. I know the ridicule you have borne on your husband's behalf.

RENÉE PÉLAGIE: Don't patronize me, Doctor. I hold you in no less contempt than I do my husband.

DR. ROYER-COLLARD: Me? But why?

RENÉE PÉLAGIE: Last night's episode was completely avoidable. If only you'd remained true to our contract.

DR. ROYER-COLLARD: I beg your pardon?

RENÉE PÉLAGIE: Was it your immediate intention to swindle me? Or did the plot dawn on you slowly, over time, like a gathering thundercloud?

DR. ROYER-COLLARD: I'm afraid I don't follow.

RENÉE PÉLAGIE: At your insistence, sir, I provided the necessary funds for a host of refurbishments.

(She pulls out a list, and reads.)

Thirty-three brass hospital beds, each fitted with restraints, twelve branding irons, a bed of nails, a set of steel-tipped martinets, and, finally, a St. Andrew's cross. And have you purchased even a single item? No!

DR. ROYER-COLLARD: I can say, with the utmost sincerity, that every franc you've given me has been put to sterling use.

RENÉE PÉLAGIE: Perhaps I have a suspicious mind, Doctor. But that fortress you're constructing on the southern edge of town . . .

DR. ROYER-COLLARD: What of it?

RENÉE PÉLAGIE: Well, people talk. Mirrors made from Venetian glass. Walls covered with Chinese silk. A balustrade pilfered from a Russian palace . . .

DR. ROYER-COLLARD: Surely you recognize that my success in these halls is contingent upon my comfort. And that my *comfort*, in turn, depends on my *surroundings*. Every stone laid, each ounce of mortar spread, each molded crest abutting each window frame hastens your husband's recovery!

RENÉE PÉLAGIE: You must admit it's odd. Your poor hospital can't even afford a whipping post. And all the while you sit at home sipping Fumé Blanc on a Grecian divan. . . .

DR. ROYER-COLLARD: I am appalled, madame, to see a woman of your standing stoop to crass innuendo.

RENÉE PÉLAGIE: Either the Ministry rewards you with a king's ransom or someone has his fingers in my till!

DR. ROYER-COLLARD: You would enter my office, sally up to my desk, and accuse me of common thievery?

RENÉE PÉLAGIE: I wouldn't call it "common," sir. Impudent. Shameless. Bald. But never "common!"

DR. ROYER-COLLARD: This room has played host to the most caustic minds. Still, I've never been so insulted.

RENÉE PÉLAGIE: I urge you to take concrete action to silence my husband, or expect a second visit from my lawyer of a far graver nature than the first.

(She barrels for the door, then turns with a flourish.)

Good day, sir!

Scene 2

COULMIER, DR. ROYER-COLLARD, THE MARQUIS.

COULMIER: The fire in the belfry has been doused. We quieted the horses in the stables. And the patients have all been firmly strapped back into their beds. Call me a fool, but I hope that you've summoned me this morning to relay *good* news.

DR. ROYER-COLLARD: You're a fool.

COULMIER: Touché.

DR. ROYER-COLLARD: Your failure has cost an innocent life.

COULMIER: I beg your pardon?

DR. ROYER-COLLARD: The seamstress, Madeleine Leclerc.

COULMIER: Madeleine . . . dead?

DR. ROYER-COLLARD: Last night, in the melee, the inmate Bouchon burst the confines of his cell and tortured the poor child until she expired.

COULMIER: *What?*

DR. ROYER-COLLARD: She was discovered this morning, splayed like a newly hung carcass, in the laundry. Bouchon was so favorably impressed by the Marquis's tale that he chose to reenact it. Lovingly, and with admirable fidelity to the author. Each laceration. Each swath of the blade.

COULMIER: Poor Madeleine! To spend her last hours at the mercy of that ham-fisted *brute*, that *ogre* . . .

DR. ROYER-COLLARD: We mustn't blaine Bouchon. If he possessed restraint . . . conscience . . . morality . . . he'd have no need of us, would he? No, the fault lies elsewhere, I'm afraid.

COULMIER: Of course.

DR. ROYER-COLLARD: It is our duty, is it not, to protect malleable minds from pernicious influence?

COULMIER: I suppose it is.

DR. ROYER-COLLARD: To admonish the individual when his habits impinge upon the safety of the whole?

COULMIER: Yes, Doctor.

DR. ROYER-COLLARD: And when we falter at this charge?

COULMIER: Bedlam, sir. And death.

DR. ROYER-COLLARD: If I seem severe to you . . . tyrannical, even . . . it's because we owe our dependents nothing less. We must provide for them what they cannot muster for themselves. *Dominion over the beast within.*

COULMIER: If you'll pardon me, Doctor, it was an endless night.

DR. ROYER-COLLARD: How many other tragedies must befall Charenton before you embrace your duty here?

COULMIER: My head has yet to touch a pillow, my lips to taste a meal—

DR. ROYER-COLLARD: Would that you had seen the girl's mother. Her face stained with tears, her eyes glazed, uncomprehending. I thank God that, because of her blindness, she was spared the sight of her daughter's riddled corpse.

COULMIER: I'll make reparation to the family.

DR. ROYER-COLLARD: There's another matter that you'd better address first.

COULMIER: Of course.

DR. ROYER-COLLARD: Might I suggest a stroll down the West Wing. Take a look at the operating theater. You'll find everything you need there.

COULMIER: That room's been locked for twenty years.

DR. ROYER-COLLARD: The douche chair, the brazier slab, the fustigator, the Procrustean bed, and the abdominal wagon. They're all at your disposal.

COULMIER: It sounds less like a hospital, Doctor, and more akin to a chamber of horrors.

DR. ROYER-COLLARD: How perceptive, Abbé.

COULMIER: Knowing my disposition toward such cruel measures . . .

(DR. ROYER-COLLARD *glares.*)

Must you . . . Mustn't we . . . Must I . . . I must . . .

(ÐR. ROYER-COLLARD *clears his throat.*)

I must have the key, sir. I've long since misplaced mine.

(DR. ROYER-COLLARD *hands* COULMIER *the key.*)

DR. ROYER-COLLARD: When you lay your head upon the pillow tonight, beg God's forgiveness for the death of poor Madeleine. You shan't have mine.

Scene 3

THE MARQUIS, COULMIER.

THE MARQUIS: Suppose one of your precious wards had attempted to walk on water and drowned. Would you condemn the Bible? I think not!

COULMIER: Would that he had only injured himself and not another.

THE MARQUIS: Am I to be held responsible for the actions of every half-wit here?

COULMIER: The man who loads the cannon and the man who fires it are both culpable, Marquis.

THE MARQUIS: It was fiction! It was not intended as how-to! Castigate Bouchon, not me.

COULMIER: Bouchon is not a man; he's an overgrown child.

THE MARQUIS: So I am to tailor my writing for imbeciles?

COULMIER: You weren't supposed to be writing at all!

THE MARQUIS: A writer cannot answer for his audience!

COULMIER: He must, when he incites it to crime!

THE MARQUIS: The experience of art, my little bull's pizzle, is a collaborative affair. The author provides the stimuli; the reader his response. All I can control is the art itself; my subject, culled from life, and told with an eye to truth, or, at least, truth as life has taught me to perceive it. And you must concede, sweetums, that life has taught me some very scabrous tidbits indeed! And so I record them! Dutifully! As any writer should! But—the response to my work. Well, poodle, that's a fickle thing indeed. It may be prompted by the reader's race! His sex! His politics! The potency of the beer he drank with dinner! The angle of his bed! *Even the last time he diddled his wife!* In short, variables well beyond the scope of the artist. What am I to do, police my readers as you police me? Ha!

COULMIER: You wish to know the sum impact of your work upon the public, Marquis?

THE MARQUIS: Pray, tell?

COULMIER: Innocent people die.

THE MARQUIS: So many authors are denied the gratification of a concrete response to their toiling. I am blessed, am I not?

COULMIER: I labored under the misconception that you felt something for the young girl. That in some dark, crusted, corroded corner of your heart she touched you.

THE MARQUIS: She was flirtatious, to me and to others.

COULMIER: Don't you dare start on that course.

THE MARQUIS: Her breasts heaving under poplin. Her ass, like two melons, bobbling at the bottom of a sack . . .

COULMIER: You'll do yourself no credit by pursuing this line.

THE MARQUIS: Bouchon has done us all a favor, nipping temptation in the bud.

COULMIER: It is no secret, Marquis, that you loved her.

THE MARQUIS: Ha!

COULMIER: It was many a time you tore a hole in your topcoat, only to secure her services!

THE MARQUIS: Rubbish!

COULMIER: You bartered pages for a single kiss.

THE MARQUIS: Who told you this?

COULMIER: You doted on her!

THE MARQUIS: Was it she?

COULMIER: You worshipped her!

THE MARQUIS: Flattering herself, I suppose!

COULMIER: *You were her slave!*

THE MARQUIS: I wanted to fuck her, that's all!

COULMIER: And did you?

THE MARQUIS: It is not your province to ask!

COULMIER: You're no stranger to rape, Marquis! And yet with her you cooed. You courted. You begged.

THE MARQUIS: Go to hell!

COULMIER: Why was it you never took her by force?

THE MARQUIS: Who is to say I did not?

COULMIER: Was it impotence?

THE MARQUIS: *Never!*

COULMIER: Was it polite deference?

THE MARQUIS: The only witness is Madeleine herself, and her lips—and her body—are sealed.

COULMIER: Was it humane regard? Was it—gasp!—*love?*

(THE MARQUIS chokes on COULMIER's last word.)

THE MARQUIS: I fucked her a thousand times! With pneumatic force!

COULMIER: We inspected the body, Marquis. She died intact.

(A stunned pause. THE MARQUIS cracks—a tiny cry at first, which erupts into genuine sobbing. Finally, he speaks. His voice is barely a whisper.)

THE MARQUIS: You will see she receives a proper burial. In the churchyard. At my expense. I implore you . . . do not inter her sweet body in the same ground as the madmen and the devils who inhabit this accursed place.

(Pause.)

COULMIER: Your terrible secret, revealed. You are a man, after all.

(THE MARQUIS looks at COULMIER for a moment. Suddenly—sharply—he spits at him. COULMIER wipes away the indignity.)

All that remains now is your punishment.

THE MARQUIS: Your lily mind cannot compete with mine in that department.

COULMIER: For that I'm grateful.

THE MARQUIS: What "frightful torture" have you devised, kitten?

COULMIER: I have knelt in the chapel and consorted with God. I have asked him if I am justified in my measures. And he has assured me that I am.

THE MARQUIS: What will it be, my little dictator?

COULMIER: Blood has been spilled and, regrettably, I must spill more to stem its ruby tide.

THE MARQUIS: The logic of a true warrior. Congratulations.

COULMIER: Don't deride me, murderer.

THE MARQUIS: Well? Don't keep me in suspense. Fifty lashes? A night on the rack?

COULMIER: Tonight you'll be . . . ah . . . you will be . . . visited by the . . .

THE MARQUIS: You haven't the stomach for this, have you?

COULMIER: I have . . . authorized . . . the procedure myself. . . .

THE MARQUIS: You haven't the balls.

COULMIER: It is our sad duty, Marquis, to . . . to . . .

THE MARQUIS: Weakling! Runt! Crab louse!

COULMIER: Oh, dear merciful God . . .

THE MARQUIS: Up in your office, buoyed by your cronies, it was easy to devise my undoing, wasn't it? *Wasn't it?* A regular parlor game. Each of you, chirping, like giddy magpies. "Solitary confinement! Perhaps we'll dock his dessert. Maybe a good spanking. Ouch!" But now, face-to-face with your victim, you're turning soft. After all, I'm not some stranger. I'm your *friend*, the Marquis.

(He extends his hand to COULMIER.*)*

I dare you. Stab my flesh. Which one of us will bleed?

(COULMIER *stares at him for a moment and takes a few paces toward the door.*)

Ha! I knew it.

COULMIER: Tonight you'll be visited by the surgeon. He'll cut out your tongue.

(*Pause.*)

THE MARQUIS: Then surely you'll grant me a final word.

COULMIER: Of course.

THE MARQUIS: I didn't forge the mind of man. Your precious God did that. Cramming it full of rancor and bloodlust. Like Zeus, thrusting all those winged demons into the tiny confines of Pandora's box. Don't hate me just because I turn the key and let them loose. "Fly, my darlings, fly! All the way to heaven, till you burst the clouds and blacken the sun!"

COULMIER: I don't hate you, Marquis. More's the pity.

(*He stands, fretful and spent. He swivels to go. Again,* THE MARQUIS *coos after him.*)

THE MARQUIS: Abbé de Coulmier.

COULMIER: What now?

(THE MARQUIS *sticks out his tongue and makes a clipping gesture.*)

THE MARQUIS: Snip, snip, snip.

(*He smiles.*)

Would that I were so easily silenced.

Scene 4

MONSIEUR PROUIX, MADAME ROYER-COLLARD,
DR. ROYER-COLLARD.

DR. ROYER-COLLARD *sits in his office. He opens a letter from* MONSIEUR
PROUIX, *and begins to read it.*

Lights rise on MONSIEUR PROUIX, *wearing a loose dressing gown. He sits
at a small writing desk and composes a note.*

MONSIEUR PROUIX: "Most Esteemed Dr. Royer-Collard, At long
last, your château is complete. You'll find everything in its assigned place: the chintz draperies, the English bellpulls, even the
ivory doorstops. Only one detail is missing. . . ."

(He emits a series of short, staccato moans, followed by a long sigh.
MADAME ROYER-COLLARD *crawls out from beneath the desk, wearing a
corset and pantaloons. She repairs her lipstick.)*

"Your wife."

(He leans down and kisses her hungrily. MADAME ROYER-COLLARD
cracks a small riding crop in the air.)

MADAME ROYER-COLLARD: You obsequious men. Underneath all
that scraping and bowing you're such wolves.

MONSIEUR PROUIX: "It would seem that, no matter how splendid
her surroundings, she cannot resist the urge to cuckold her husband."

MADAME ROYER-COLLARD: Tell him I'm no fool! A prison's still a
prison, with or without wainscoting and Baccarat chandeliers!

MONSIEUR PROUIX: "And so I have pirated Marguerite away to a safe
haven. . . ."

MADAME ROYER-COLLARD: Ooh, ooh, ooh! Tell him if he uncovers our whereabouts—

MONSIEUR PROUIX: Yes?

MADAME ROYER-COLLARD: —you'll slit your wrist with a razor! And I'll plunge a hatpin through my heart!

MONSIEUR PROUIX: You'd do that rather than forsake our love?

MADAME ROYER-COLLARD: No. But tell him I would.

(A pause. MONSIEUR PROUIX frowns.)

MONSIEUR PROUIX: I worry, Marguerite, that you don't really love me at all, but merely mean to use me to your own convenient ends, as a vehicle to escape your husband's tyranny.

MADAME ROYER-COLLARD: You're brighter than you look. Now write.

(MONSIEUR PROUIX shrugs, and obediently writes.)

MONSIEUR PROUIX: "A . . . hatpin . . . through . . . my heart . . ."

MADAME ROYER-COLLARD: Sign it quickly. Then carry me upstairs so you can ravish me again! On linens for which he so dearly paid!

MONSIEUR PROUIX: Yes, Marguerite, yes!

MADAME ROYER-COLLARD: We'll stain the bedding. We'll dampen the chamois and leave puddles of love all over the coverlet!

MONSIEUR PROUIX: On the satin twill . . . then, I beg you, on the teakwood floor of the salon . . . and please, oh, please . . . as a crowning gesture . . . on the ocelot rug in the foyer!

(As if in answer, MADAME ROYER-COLLARD yowls like a cat. MONSIEUR PROUIX signs.)

"Sincerely, Jean-Pierre Prouix."

(MADAME ROYER-COLLARD *takes the pen from his hand and adds an epithet.*)

MADAME ROYER-COLLARD: *"The . . . architect . . . of your . . . unhappy . . . fate!"*

(MONSIEUR PROUIX *smiles. He breaks into a laugh;* MADAME ROYER-COLLARD *chimes in. The lights on the couple fade.* DR. ROYER-COLLARD *sits, stalwart. He begins to tremble. Slowly, deliberately, he tears the letter into tiny shreds. Blackout.*)

Scene 5

COULMIER, DR. ROYER-COLLARD, THE MARQUIS.

COULMIER: The surgeon completed his grim task just as the sun was about to rise. So violent were the Marquis's protestations that he prolonged his own pain. I have, as you requested, proof of our success.

(COULMIER *places a small tin box on* DR. ROYER-COLLARD's *desk.*)

His tongue, Doctor. So long and serpentine I had to roll it round a dowel. Now our grisly business is concluded. We'll never again have to wield the scalpel against the Marquis, or any ward.

DR. ROYER-COLLARD: You are aware, are you not, that even the patients are laughing behind your back?

COULMIER: What?

DR. ROYER-COLLARD: How can they look to you as their savior when you inspire ridicule in lieu of respect?

COULMIER: Doctor Royer-Collard, I have fulfilled my duties and beyond. I stood, sir, at the surgeon's side, holding the Marquis fast to his chair, my knees weak and my head swimming, all in the service of Charenton. Now, I refuse to be further baited or debased.

DR. ROYER-COLLARD: Do you know the condition of his room, Abbé?

COULMIER: His room?

DR. ROYER-COLLARD: Words!

COULMIER: Words?

DR. ROYER-COLLARD: Everywhere, words! On the ceiling. Written on the floor. Etched on the walls. A phantasmagoria of words.

COULMIER: No! No! No, no, no, no . . .

DR. ROYER-COLLARD: All in his unmistakable script!

COULMIER: But *how?*

DR. ROYER-COLLARD: He spat into his own excrement and formed a kind of paint.

COULMIER: No, dear God, please . . .

DR. ROYER-COLLARD: Finally, a medium worthy of his art. With his fingers, like a child, he decorated the room with language.

COULMIER: Has he no shred of decency?

DR. ROYER-COLLARD: I mustered the patience to follow its scrawl, and found this dense verbiage contained a story.

COULMIER: So the stench of this tale is twofold. . . .

DR. ROYER-COLLARD: It plunges so deep into the acrid chambers of man's aching heart that even the angels are left to weep, and the saints to gasp for air.

(COULMIER *is sobbing, at his wits' end.*)

COULMIER: Don't make me hear it! I beg you!

(Lights rise on THE MARQUIS. *He sits impassive, his lips sewn together. All around him, covering every inch of wall space, is language. Oozing out of each crack, each crevice. Dripping from the ceiling. Lining the floor. We hear his voice.)*

THE VOICE OF THE MARQUIS: And now, at last, an innocuous tale, sans all perversion, designed to appease my Puritanical captors.

DR. ROYER-COLLARD: A hollow promise, offered so the story's final twist will shock us all the more.

THE VOICE OF THE MARQUIS: Monsieur LaFarge was hopelessly smitten by a pretty young maid named Marie Duplaix. He'd long sought her hand in marriage. But each time he proposed she refused. In hopes of winning her love, Monsieur LaFarge employed the services of a famous tailor. "You must design a wedding gown," he told the tailor, "of such stumptuousness and splendor that, for the privilege of wearing it, Marie will become my bride." The tailor bid Marie choose from a host of fabrics. "Kind sir," she cried, "I wish to try them all!" Finally, she alighted on a royal velvet, more costly than a peau de soie or Belgian lace. The tailor drove his needle through the soft fabric, in and out, in and out, in and out, in and out until the dress was done. Marie slipped it on before the glass. The gorgeous gown softened her brittle heart, and so she consented to wed.

(There is a pause. COULMIER *is waiting for the voice of* THE MARQUIS *to continue.)*

COULMIER: That's it? That's all?

*(*THE MARQUIS *breaks into a hideous smile through his stitches.)*

THE VOICE OF THE MARQUIS: Voilà. Happily ever after. The end.

(Lights fade on THE MARQUIS.*)*

COULMIER: But there's no debauch. No nefarious carousal . . .

DR. ROYER-COLLARD: Don't you see? He's trumped us! He's masked his obscenity with metaphor!

COULMIER: He has?

DR. ROYER-COLLARD: Monsieur LaFarge wants to secure the heart of a winsome young thing. So what does he do? He unwittingly hires his own rival!

COULMIER: He does?

DR. ROYER-COLLARD: Of course! The tailor!

COULMIER: The tailor?

DR. ROYER-COLLARD: I can almost see the two of them. Marie, all dewy and pink in her crinolines. The tailor, measuring tape in hand, pulling it taut across her heaving breasts . . .

COULMIER: Does the Marquis provide such a description?

DR. ROYER-COLLARD: Oh, no. He's become far too skilled for that. He leaves us hanging with a few vague phrases. We're forced to supply our own salacious detail!

COULMIER: But that's preposterous! This tale is nothing but a senti-mental romance, as toothless as it is predictable.

DR. ROYER-COLLARD: Don't be so *naive*, Abbé! The story ripples with innuendo! Note Marie's fickle nature. She can't choose a single fabric, no. She begs to try them all! A sly allusion to her promiscuity. She is clearly a nymphomaniac, as inconstant in her taste in men as she is in clothing.

COULMIER: She is?

DR. ROYER-COLLARD: And mark her exorbitance! Royal velvet! How, pray tell, will LaFarge afford such luxury? She intends to ruin him! To drive him to crime!

COULMIER: She does?

DR. ROYER-COLLARD: Embezzlement, perhaps, or fraud!

COULMIER: I fear, Doctor, that you've strayed too far from the source—

DR. ROYER-COLLARD: Choose any line of text, and beneath its harmless veneer you'll find nothing but sin and degeneracy! Go ahead! *I dare you!*

COULMIER: "The tailor drove the needle through the soft fabric, in and out, in and out, in and out, in and out—"

DR. ROYER-COLLARD: Aha! There! You see!

COULMIER: Good heavens. It's as plain as day, isn't it?

DR. ROYER-COLLARD: *Copulation!*

COULMIER: One or two well-chosen words and you can almost see them coupling.

DR. ROYER-COLLARD: Rutting like a pair of dogs! Her robust thighs, parted—

COULMIER: Her mossy crevice, revealed—

DR. ROYER-COLLARD: The battering of his mighty ram—

COULMIER: The enveloping lips of her virginal cavity—

DR. ROYER-COLLARD: The soft, insistent slapping of skin against skin—

COULMIER: Her lewd shrieks as he plunges deep into the warm sepulcher of her woman-flesh!

DR. ROYER-COLLARD: It's all there, Abbé! Lurking beneath his seemingly flaccid prose!

COULMIER: Why, the roué! The poltroon!

DR. ROYER-COLLARD: Exhaustion overtook the Marquis, and so his script tapers. But surely you can divine the story's conclusion!

COULMIER: I can?

DR. ROYER-COLLARD: Once wed, the young bride abandons her husband and decamps with her rapist!

COULMIER: No!

(DR. ROYER-COLLARD slams his fists against the desk.)

DR. ROYER-COLLARD: The strumpet! The scurrilous little tramp! She ought to be boiled! She ought to be hoisted on a pike!

COULMIER: Surely we could posit other outcomes. . . .

DR. ROYER-COLLARD: In the world of the Marquis, what other possibilities exist? *Only catastrophe.*

(He sinks into his chair, his chest concave.)

Poor, gullible LaFarge. He offered everything to the duplicitous little snit. His unwavering devotion. High social station. An opulent home, no doubt, with Italian tile, and a garden full of imported tulips . . .

(Tentatively, COULMIER reaches to touch DR. ROYER-COLLARD's shoulder, to comfort him.)

COULMIER: Shh . . . Doctor . . .

DR. ROYER-COLLARD: And what did she proffer instead? Nothing but heartbreak. Now LaFarge is left alone. His love lost. His reputation past repair. His very post in jeopardy.

COULMIER: I can't help noticing that this particular tale has affected you more than the rest.

DR. ROYER-COLLARD: Though I'm loath to admit it, as a result of his persistence, his writing has improved. It now boasts a certain . . . prescience . . . it didn't have before.

(He sighs a final sigh, then regains his severe demeanor.)

You may pack your bags, Abbé. A carriage awaits, ready to transport you a great distance from Saint-Maurice.

COULMIER: What's this?

DR. ROYER-COLLARD: I've arranged for your reassignment to a monastery in Avignon. There, rather than tending the infirm, you'll transcribe huge Latin tomes by candlelight.

COULMIER: With no warning, Doctor? No chance for reprieve?

DR. ROYER-COLLARD: I am tendering my resignation to the Ministry, effective immediately.

COULMIER: You too, Doctor?

DR. ROYER-COLLARD: It's preemptive, Abbé. I was entrusted to forge order from chaos, and what has transpired since my arrival here? Murder and mayhem—events which, regrettably, do little to enhance my curriculum vitae. I prefer to exit with grace, rather than have my job wrested from me in what would undoubtedly prove to be a rather conclusive study in the art of humiliation.

COULMIER: But what of Charenton?

DR. ROYER-COLLARD: I am recommending to the Ministry that we close her doors forever.

COULMIER: But why, I beseech you?

DR. ROYER-COLLARD: *We don't govern Charenton—he does!* We flatter ourselves his superiors, when in truth we dangle from his strings!

COULMIER: What of the patients? They've no place to go. No manner in which to clothe and nourish themselves.

DR. ROYER-COLLARD: We'll turn them loose upon the streets. They have learned the Marquis's maxims. Now, let them live by his commandments. Let them kill for their trousers; let them rip bread and meat from the hands of children.

COULMIER: Don't you see, Doctor? To admit defeat is to endorse his philosophy!

DR. ROYER-COLLARD: Then so be it.

COULMIER: I cannot and will not accept these terms. *He has yet to conquer me!*

DR. ROYER-COLLARD: That's enough, Abbé! Now go. Before the coachman leaves without you.

COULMIER: The principles we espouse here, the ideals we embrace, are the very rudiments of Christian thought! They have weathered the centuries, and cast the world in its present shape! And the Marquis . . . Ha! He's nothing but a pustule on the face of history! Stand him on a pedestal next to Christ and you will see—he is a puny creature!

(He falls to his knees before DR. ROYER-COLLARD.*)*

I implore you, sir, give me one more chance. I must see him quelled. Otherwise I shall never again have the courage to face the glass.

(A long pause.)

DR. ROYER-COLLARD: Very well. Since you insist . . .

COULMIER: I offer all my gratitude, and place my reputation at your feet.

DR. ROYER-COLLARD: Hold fast to your noble purpose. To revenge the death of a helpless child. To preserve the sanctity of Charenton.

COULMIER: To keep our gates open, and our chambers full.

DR. ROYER-COLLARD: Go, then, and do as your heart commands you!

Scene 6

COULMIER, THE MARQUIS.

COULMIER: A verbose insult, Marquis!

(He gestures to the words that cover THE MARQUIS*'s room.)*

The snide carping of a jaded bombast! A cruel satire of conventional mores! And masked as a harmless love story! This time, python, you won't slither past!

*(*THE MARQUIS, *sans tongue, tries to protest.)*

The story's true tone lies between the lines, not in them! That's plain to see, my friend. What do you take me for? A dolt? I swore I'd confiscate your implements, whatever they might be! Place your hands upon the block. On the block! Now! Ten venomous quills, each dripping its own poison!

*(*THE MARQUIS *places his hands upon the block.)*

What else might you employ as your stylus? Tell me that you'll hold a stick in your teeth and I'll have each molar plucked. Your toes, perhaps and I'll crack them from the joints. And—yes, oh yes—lest we forget. Your tireless tool, which when engorged might play the role of plume! That I'll circle round a gear, then yank it from its fleshly moorings! Well, sir? Tell me!

*(*THE MARQUIS, *frantic, begins to scribble in the dirt.* COULMIER *reads.)*

"One . . . last . . . request. A . . . dying man's . . . plea."

*(*THE MARQUIS *stares at* COULMIER *hopefully.)*

What is it you want?

(THE MARQUIS *goes back to his scratching. Again,* COULMIER *deciphers the line.*)

"Take my manhood last . . . so I might savor . . . the torture . . . till the end. . . ."

(COULMIER *kicks* THE MARQUIS *in the stomach.*)

Down, Satan's scribe!

(COULMIER *yanks* THE MARQUIS's *head back and intones in his face.*)

This time we'll not waste the surgeon's skills. For such crude cutting, the butcher will suffice!

(*A sudden blackout. In the darkness, such sounds! Gears turning. Muscles snapping. The whoosh of a blade through air, and the crunch when it meets its target. The crack of bone and the popping of joints. The low creak of limbs being stretched. All this, of course, accompanied by appropriate human exclamations. The sounds accumulate, becoming a kind of demented symphony.*)

Scene 7

COULMIER, DR. ROYER-COLLARD.

COULMIER *places a matching pair of tin boxes before* DR. ROYER-COLLARD.

COULMIER: In this box you'll find his right hand. In this, his left. No longer will they fashion quills from refuse.

(*He places a second set of boxes before* DR. ROYER-COLLARD.)

In this box you'll find his right foot. In this, its mate. He won't be teaching those nimble toes to write.

(*He places a fifth box before* DR. ROYER-COLLARD.)

And last, but not least, the font of his imaginings. In this last box, his tally, whacked.

DR. ROYER-COLLARD: My, my. You have exceeded my expectations.

COULMIER: And my own.

DR. ROYER-COLLARD: And how is the patient faring?

COULMIER: Poorly. At each extremity, a new wound. To look at him. Doctor, is to see the shape of a man etched in bandages.

DR. ROYER-COLLARD: And you? It must've been an ordeal.

COULMIER: At first it was unbearable.

DR. ROYER-COLLARD: And then?

COULMIER: As you know, the mind serves its owner with surprising elasticity. Though repulsed, I was fueled by the necessity of my actions. And my horror hardened into resolve. Steel purpose. I felt a growing . . . interest . . . in the proceedings.

DR. ROYER-COLLARD: Oh?

COULMIER: I no longer averted my gaze. One box, then two. With austere ceremony, the butcher filled each tiny tomb with tissue and bone. From deep within my core, a quiver. A jolt.

DR. ROYER-COLLARD: Yes?

COULMIER: A certain . . . satisfaction . . . knowing with each chop . . . I was taking a step closer to God.

DR. ROYER-COLLARD: So tell me. Will you sleep soundly tonight?

COULMIER: No, sir. Plainly put, I never expect to sleep again.

(*A brief pause.*)

And you?

DR. ROYER-COLLARD: I worry that our task is not complete.

COULMIER: I beg your pardon?

(DR. ROYER-COLLARD *taps a finger knowingly on his own forehead.*)

DR. ROYER-COLLARD: His most potent organ remains intact.

COULMIER: Please, he's been well hacked! I left him more meat than man!

DR. ROYER-COLLARD: Still . . .

COULMIER: He flails about on the floor of his cell like some pitiful starfish!

DR. ROYER-COLLARD: You've broken his body, true. But what about his mind? For all we know, it still composes. What will his next story be, Abbé? Perhaps a tale about a timorous priest . . .

COULMIER: I dare say, Doctor, we can't control his thoughts. We can only mute their expression.

DR. ROYER-COLLARD: Then we have not truly cured him, have we?

COULMIER: What murderous act would you have me commit?

DR. ROYER-COLLARD: Finish the job you've begun.

COULMIER: These hands cannot . . . will not . . . extinguish life.

DR. ROYER-COLLARD: I had hoped they were the hands of a hero.

COULMIER: You've hands of your own. Why not use them? Why let a minion perform the deed and usurp the glory? Or do you, too, fear the stains?

DR. ROYER-COLLARD: You've done the worst. The rest is mere formality.

COULMIER: Goodbye, Doctor. I'll spend one final night in my quarters here, and tomorrow set out for regions beyond.

DR. ROYER-COLLARD: He lies there nobbled, fermenting in his own filth. One breath away from salvation. It's in your power to deliver him safely there.

COULMIER: I've given my answer; it won't change.

DR. ROYER-COLLARD: Abandon Charenton and you abandon God.

COULMIER: I pray that fate never again ushers me through these portals or casts my shadow against your door.

Scene 8

COULMIER, THE GHOST OF MADELEINE, THE MARQUIS.

The charnel house.

COULMIER *kneels before the casket containing the body of* MADELEINE.

COULMIER: Before I take my leave, a final tarry here. To beg forgiveness, dear Madeleine, for your unkind end. Dear God, pity me! Hold her fast by your side, so that in heaven we might be reunited. There I shall fall to my knees and beg her mercy evermore.

(He leans over to kiss the coffin. It opens. MADELEINE *bolts upright. Her body has been restored; there's no trace of the horror that befell her at the end of Act One. Her body is bathed in a celestial glow. The trills of an angelic chorus waft through the air.)*

MADELEINE: Oh, Abbé! Freed at last from this pine box! Unearthed by your pleas!

COULMIER: What's this? Sweet Madeleine's specter?

(He falls to his knees. He takes MADELEINE'*s hand and presses her palm to his cheek.)*

You're an angel, aren't you, sent to deliver me? I've committed such inhuman, such appalling acts. . . . Tell me I've still some small hope of redemption.

MADELEINE: When I was stabbéd through and through by the madman Bouchon, I fell into the very darkest slumber. When I awoke, I was nestled in the bosom of our Lord Jesus Christ. It was as if the very earth had risen in the shape of a man and gathered me in its tender embrace.

(The walls split, and a resplendent figure of Christ appears, portrayed by none other than THE MARQUIS.*)*

"Savior," I whispered, too awed to speak any louder. "If only you would kiss my wounds and make them heal." And so he did. When his lips met the gash on my cheek, the flesh closed, new and rosy. When he pecked the bruise on my knee, it was gone. Soon my body was again pristine, each mark of the lunatic's blade abolished. But alas, sir. Christ's potent kisses did not cease. His mouth no longer sought my lesions; it went after sweeter fruit.

COULMIER: What impiety is this?

MADELEINE: "Oh, Holy One," cried I, crossing my legs to thwart his advance, "I am not injured there!"

THE MARQUIS: "You've so often worshipped at my temple—"

MADELEINE: —was his reply—

THE MARQUIS: "That now I long to worship yours."

COULMIER: Mademoiselle, if you wish to be spared the tortures of hell, then cease this abomination!

MADELEINE: I merely report these events! I am not their agent! And then—oh, Abbé! It was then I saw the mask slip from its perch upon his nose. This was no Son of God but his inverse.

(The figure of Christ swivels his mask; now he is Satan.)

THE MARQUIS: There is no God but me!

MADELEINE: And then Satan parted his vestments to reveal his carnal staff.

COULMIER: I'll have no more of this ghastly tale!

MADELEINE: How it defied biology! Less like the fountain of man and more fitting to a sea serpent! Such tentacles! Yes, 'tis true! His wand was *triple-pronged!*

THE MARQUIS: The Father, the Son, and the Holy Ghost!

MADELEINE: With that blood-engorged Trinity, he plumbed my throat, my matrix, and that narrowest of strictures which Nature most conceals! My every breach was corked! The Devil's hot rain shot through me like quicksilver!

THE MARQUIS: *In nomine Patris et Filii et Spiritu Sanctu. Amen.*

(The walls close on the figure of Satan. MADELEINE's *voice is now the voice of a skilled seductress.)*

MADELEINE: When my legs were opened, so were my eyes. Ooh, Abbé! Now in death I can freely taste what in life modesty so cruelly forbade.

COULMIER: You are not Madeleine! You're nothing but a succubus, disguised!

(During the following passages, MADELEINE *strokes* COULMIER *gently, her hands wandering across his body like moths along a wall. In spite of his best efforts to the contrary,* COULMIER *is steadily aroused.)*

MADELEINE: How you sucked me from death with a single kiss on the lid of my coffin! What other tricks does that sweet mouth know?

COULMIER: Unhand me, I beg you.

MADELEINE: Don't you like my touch?

COULMIER: There are vows more potent than man's primal stirrings. . . .

MADELEINE: Vows? To whom?

COULMIER: To God.

MADELEINE: What God?

COULMIER: The one you have so clearly forsaken.

MADELEINE: Oh, Abbé. What a solid ridge of bone. I'll draw it slowly into my own thin fissure. There, in a velvet vice, I'll milk it dry.

COULMIER: I beseech you, not there. . . .

(He is inflamed.)

MADELEINE: Tell me, beloved. Who needs your God now?

(She seizes COULMIER *and kisses him. He breaks away urgently; his resistance is spent.)*

COULMIER: All right then, witch. I'll speak to you in the only language that you know. I'll drive my own stake through your wretched center and pin you forever in the grave.

(He thrusts MADELEINE *into the coffin and climbs atop her. Suddenly, in his arms, she goes limp. Her body is still, and breathless.)*

What's this? All breath left her body? Oh, God. Her limbs . . . the stench of her flesh . . .

(He shrinks back from the casket, horrified.)

Spirit! Answer me! Did the Marquis bid you to visit me, or did you burst unchecked from my own brain? Tell me, I beg you! Has he so long polluted me that my own demons are now dislodged?

*(*COULMIER *slams the lid of the coffin shut with urgent resolve.)*

I am a priest. I don't have the capacity for such heresy.

*(*COULMIER *beats both fists on the lid of the casket. He looks heavenward and asks with murderous intensity.)*

Whose fantasy was this? Whose?

Scene 9

COULMIER, THE MARQUIS.

By now, of course, THE MARQUIS *is in a state of hideous disrepair.* COUL-
MIER *prays quietly.*

COULMIER: Dear Heavenly Father. I could not render this last act if
it weren't for the knowledge that I'll be setting this pagan free.
That he will be liberated from a society he deems monstrous in
design; and that, in turn, all France shall be free from his perdi-
tion. And so, with a single, tiny blow, let a greater good flourish
from this grisly command.

*(*COULMIER *stands. He turns gently to* THE MARQUIS.*)*

Your head, my poor, misguided man, upon the block.

*(Blackout. A loud thwarp, followed by a wrenching tear. Next, a long roll,
like a heavy ball cascading down an incline. Finally, a dull thud.)*

Scene 10

RENÉE PÉLAGIE, DR. ROYER-COLLARD.

Newly atop DR. ROYER-COLLARD*'s desk, a tin box large enough to contain a human head. It rests heavily in the room, like an evil portent.* DR.
ROYER-COLLARD *sits behind it.*

RENÉE PÉLAGIE *enters, in resplendent dress.*

RENÉE PÉLAGIE: Good heavens, Doctor! Swing open the shutters!
Never did heaven proffer a more beauteous morn!

DR. ROYER-COLLARD: Darkness befits the day's solemnity, madame.

RENÉE PÉLAGIE: I haven't much time. Madame Miramond had me to breakfast in her garden this morning—oh, such a meal! Plum rosettes floating in cognac, profiteroles bursting with cream, braised ham shank, steamed rhododendrons—it's all I can do to stand! And tonight, mon Dieu!, it's off to Paris! To the opera! An opening! Commissioned by none other than Empress Josephine! My confidante and occasional paramour, the dear Monsieur Baudoin, has given me a ruby tiara to commemorate the occasion!

(She dissolves into giggles of delight.)

Yes, it's me! It's truly me! Renée Pélagie Cordier de Montreuil! The toast of France!

DR. ROYER-COLLARD: Your social schedule has markedly improved.

RENÉE PÉLAGIE: Indeed it has! My days have become one endless fete, each dancing into the next without pause. And I have you to thank for it!

DR. ROYER-COLLARD: Is it because we have once and for all silenced your husband's muse?

RENÉE PÉLAGIE: On the contrary. It's because he has received such atrocious treatment at your hands.

DR. ROYER-COLLARD: What's this?

RENÉE PÉLAGIE: He's turned from monster to martyr overnight. There are those who swear that your actions against my husband exceeded his prose.

DR. ROYER-COLLARD: I don't believe it!

RENÉE PÉLAGIE: You know how people gossip. "Did you hear? They bled the Marquis with a hundred leeches!" Or better still, "They broke his fingers, so he couldn't hold his quill!" Why, it smacks of the Terror! The story currently in circulation . . . *l' histoire du moment . . .* it's too absurd, really, you'll think me daft . . . is that the Marquis—once an able-bodied man—*has been disassembled!* Don't blanch, Doctor! It's ludicrous, I know! They say he lies in seven separate—

(She takes note of the boxes strewing the desk. She counts them. She gasps, then turns white.)

Oh, good God!

(DR. ROYER-COLLARD begins to fervently argue in his own defense.)

DR. ROYER-COLLARD: Recall your desperation! The poignancy of your call to see him stifled! We did your bidding, nothing more.

RENÉE PÉLAGIE: *My* bidding, sir? I bade you kill the author—not the man!

DR. ROYER-COLLARD: If our measures seem extreme . . . unortho-dox . . . well, so was the patient.

RENÉE PÉLAGIE: Yes. Indeed. That he was. . . .

DR. ROYER-COLLARD: I pray that you see the necessity of our action here. And that you will one day—when your grief abates—commend the wisdom which prescribed so conclusive a remedy.

(RENÉE PÉLAGIE gingerly advances toward the desk. Mustering her courage, she gazes at each box, one by one. When she reaches the box containing THE MARQUIS's head, she stops.)

RENÉE PÉLAGIE: I don't dare ask. Is this—

DR. ROYER-COLLARD: It is.

(RENÉE PÉLAGIE reaches out a quivering hand. With sudden resolve, she plants it firmly on the lid of the box and lets out a tremulous sigh.)

RENÉE PÉLAGIE: It's been countless years since I stood in the same room as my husband. This is not quite the reunion I had imag-ined.

(Her eyes well with tears.)

If you please, sir. Grant a grieving widow a moment alone with the piteous remains of her decimated spouse.

DR. ROYER-COLLARD: As you wish, madame.

(He graciously steps into the recesses of his office. RENÉE PÉLAGIE *touches her hand to her lips, then presses a kiss on the top of the box.)*

RENÉE PÉLAGIE: My dear Donatien. If, as penance for the life you've lived, you now find yourself in the blackest corner of hell . . . be consoled, my darling. You're the only man in the world who might find heaven there.

(She steps away from the doctor's desk and dabs her eyes. DR. ROYER-COLLARD *steps out of the shadows.)*

DR. ROYER-COLLARD: I must ask you to be plain with me. Do you intend legal action against the asylum for the loss of your husband?

RENÉE PÉLAGIE: Don't be absurd. I owe you lasting appreciation. My star, already on the rise, will soon pierce the stratosphere! I expect to dine out on his name and your barbarity for some time. My only regret is that this turnabout may cost you dearly.

DR. ROYER-COLLARD: How so, madame?

RENÉE PÉLAGIE: As you can well imagine, people will not be predisposed to offer their support to a hospital so sorely besmirched.

DR. ROYER-COLLARD: I hope crass public sentiment won't inhibit your own generosity. After all, we did put a rather definitive end to your plight.

RENÉE PÉLAGIE: Doctor, please. Every bank note I tendered would be soaked in my husband's blood.

DR. ROYER-COLLARD: Yes. Of course. Forgive my impertinence.

RENÉE PÉLAGIE: It's one of life's cruel ironies, I suppose, that success for one must always come at the price of another. *C'est la vie!*

(She heads for the door. She turns.)

Oh, Doctor. Please don't think me forward, but I was aggrieved to hear about your wife. Her rather . . . inexplicable . . . disappearance. The thought of you, abandoned in that expansive house, shuffling down those endless corridors. Dining solo in that colossal banquet hall. It rattles my heart.

DR. ROYER-COLLARD: Your capacity to empathize, madame, almost defies plausibility.

RENÉE PÉLAGIE: And now I must be off. I mustn't keep the coachmen waiting. They'll turn randy in the heat, and I'll have no choice but to appease them!

(She turns beet red.)

Oh, dear! How lovely to blush for *pleasurable* reasons!

(She turns wistful.)

Only yesterday I attended a christening. A christening! From "Satan's Bride" to "Godmother" in one fell swoop!

(With a flourish, she charges toward the exit.)

Society may be a capricious mistress, but in me she has found a most willing slave! Ta-ta!

(And she is gone. DR. ROYER-COLLARD *sits, ashen.)*

Scene 11

COULMIER, DR. ROYER-COLLARD.

COULMIER *enters.*

He carries a small valise, packed with his belongings.

COULMIER: My job is done. I'll be leaving for the coast tomorrow morning.

DR. ROYER-COLLARD: What's this?

COULMIER: Charenton is a place for healing. I am no longer fit to walk its halls. In Nature's embrace, I hope to rediscover my true constitution.

(He goes for the door.)

DR. ROYER-COLLARD: You can't leave, my friend. Not now.

COULMIER: Why not?

DR. ROYER-COLLARD: I . . . ah . . . I have spoken with the Ministry.

COULMIER: And?

DR. ROYER-COLLARD: They question our course here.

COULMIER: We accomplished our primary aim. We ceased production of his repulsive prose.

DR. ROYER-COLLARD: But the cost was somewhat . . . in their minds . . . drastic. Radicals, ignorant of the facts, have leaped to some rather incriminating conclusions.

COULMIER: Such as? . . .

DR. ROYER-COLLARD: That we . . . that you . . . were less than humane.

COULMIER: I did nothing without your sanction!

DR. ROYER-COLLARD: Please, Abbé.

COULMIER: *What?*

DR. ROYER-COLLARD: You know that's not true.

COULMIER: You incited my every action!

DR. ROYER-COLLARD: The Marquis incited your action, not I.

COULMIER: It was you who cried, "He must be silenced, damn the means!"

DR. ROYER-COLLARD: A night on the rack, yes! Maybe a spin on the wheel! But *vivisection?*

COULMIER: Did your urging ever falter?

DR. ROYER-COLLARD: Circumstances have turned you surly. Interred too long with the beast, you've now become one.

COULMIER: If I am a vicious cur, then you are surely my master.

DR. ROYER-COLLARD: In point of fact, I never touched him.

COULMIER: I'll speak to the Ministry myself.

DR. ROYER-COLLARD: The surgeon and the butcher have already testified on my behalf.

COULMIER: And what did those turncoats spew?

DR. ROYER-COLLARD: That I never ordained your gruesome measures. And that during their enactment I was absent, while you stood by, instructing each dissection. It was even remarked that in one instance, overcome by zest, you pirated a finger bone to wear, concealed, round your neck.

COULMIER: Slander! Perjury! Lies! Let them judge me by my intentions, not by the acts themselves. Violence in pursuit of pleasure is one thing. In pursuit of justice, it's another.

DR. ROYER-COLLARD: And how do you hope to be judged?

COULMIER: As one who defended the public good!

DR. ROYER-COLLARD: The thrill was a mere dividend?

(This stops COULMIER *cold.)*

COULMIER: It's true.

DR. ROYER-COLLARD: Forgive me.

COULMIER: When I ordered the surgeon to sever his tongue, I was green, a novice. But when I came for his head, I did so with all the calm malevolence of a Sadean protagonist. Afterward . . . consumed by guilt . . . I sought to pay for his flesh with my own.

(He loosens his vestments. His back and chest are a maze of scars, some old, others newly applied.)

DR. ROYER-COLLARD: That's enough.

COULMIER: I took a cane to my back. Soon my skin toughened and withstood the lashing. And so I sought the knife. "Surely," I thought, "if I can weather pain equal to that which I inflicted . . . I will be forgiven." But with each new gash Christ offered me a sly reward. Such exquisite stings . . .

DR. ROYER-COLLARD: Clothe yourself. Now.

COULMIER: I can't stop. My body has become a map of suffering, and I am its obsessed cartographer. I have stared into the face of evil, Doctor. And . . . heaven help me, please . . . I have never seen such terrible beauty. Who have I become? What am I to do in my defense?

(Tenderly, DR. ROYER-COLLARD *restores* COULMIER's *robe.)*

DR. ROYER-COLLARD: That will take care of itself in time.

COULMIER: But how?

DR. ROYER-COLLARD: We intend to publish the Marquis's manuscripts.

COULMIER: I beg your pardon?

DR. ROYER-COLLARD: Anonymously, of course. We need not divulge Charenton's name.

COULMIER: That is the very calamity we sought to prevent!

DR. ROYER-COLLARD: And now it is our only recourse.

COULMIER: Recourse against *what*?

DR. ROYER-COLLARD: Against our ruination. Our revenues have dropped precipitously. We have not fed our wards for three days. Even the dogs scavenge. With profits from the sale of his books, we'll establish a trust in perpetuity. Charenton will rise like the proverbial phoenix. We'll never again be forced to rely on the fickle allegiance of smug, self-righteous philanthropists.

COULMIER: I'll burn his writings myself in a pyre, before I let them pass from this place.

(DR. ROYER-COLLARD *approaches* COULMIER *and takes him gently by the shoulders, sitting him down.*)

DR. ROYER-COLLARD: Think, my boy. The Marquis's own writings are your best rationale. Surely anyone who reads the pollution inscribed therein will thank you for purging its creator.

COULMIER: Why, yes. Yes, of course.

DR. ROYER-COLLARD: A limited edition. The obsessive patients will set the type, and the listless ones can do the binding. Exorbitantly priced, to preclude the riffraff.

COULMIER: No. No, I beseech you. In every home, a copy. Let mothers yank their children round and read his prose with hearty voices.

(He stares, unwavering, at DR. ROYER-COLLARD.)

Let his volume lie by every Bible as its inverse.

DR. ROYER-COLLARD: And why not? Two sides of the same coin. The first book as reviled as the second is sacred.

*(*COULMIER *breaks into a smile. He starts to giggle. His laughter teeters on the brink of desperation.)*

COULMIER: We're left with a riddle, aren't we, Doctor?

DR. ROYER-COLLARD: A riddle?

COULMIER: Which book tells the truth about mankind, and which lies?

*(*DR. ROYER-COLLARD, *uncomfortable, shifts his gaze. He picks up the tin box containing* THE MARQUIS*'s head.)*

DR. ROYER-COLLARD: Might I suggest that we make a gift of his skull to the Phrenology Laboratory. They can, I'm certain, divine from its cranial shape those features exclusive to the libertine. What crests of bone distinguish monsters from men. From you, Abbé. Or me.

COULMIER: Let them conduct their experiments with all due haste. I need . . . proof, Doctor . . . proof positive for the sake of my soul . . . I am not of his ilk!

DR. ROYER-COLLARD: When the lab provides its findings, then I'm certain you shall be released.

COULMIER: Released?

(A fast blackout, followed by the rumbling echo of a door as it slams . . . the turning of a padlock.)

Scene 12

COULMIER.

COULMIER *paces in the cell formerly occupied by* THE MARQUIS.

COULMIER: Valcour! *Pssst, Valcour!* I have such horrendous truths to impart! And no one in the world to tell them to!

(He presses his face against the bars and whispers urgently.)

At the edge of the earth . . . on her last precipice . . . where rock cuts into the night sky . . . there are no angels to guide us . . . no devils to lead us astray. Would that there were! Alas, there's only the lone figure of a man, swirling endlessly in a hollow void!

(He has a sudden thought.)

I beseech you, bring me paper! I'll need reams of parchment, and gallons of ink besides! Valcour! Valcour . . .

(Lights remain, dimly, on COULMIER *in his cell.)*

Scene 13

THE MARQUIS, COULMIER.

The six tin boxes containing THE MARQUIS*'s tongue, his hands, his feet, and his member still sit upon the desk.*

The largest box, containing his head, lies beneath the desk, on the floor.

A tapping sound. It grows more insistent. One of the boxes opens. Tentatively, a severed hand emerges. It explores the desk. Finally, it alights on a second box and opens it. Out pops its mate.

Together they twiddle their thumbs.

The box on the floor begins to rattle. It shakes like a jack-in-the-box about to pop. The clasp jiggles free, and the box falls open, revealing the dismembered head of THE MARQUIS.

The head glances up to discover the hands. It speaks.

THE MARQUIS'S HEAD: Ah, my beauties! I knew you'd never desert me! Look. There. On the desk. Sheaves of paper . . . an inkwell . . . and a ready quill!

(One hand picks up the quill, while the other readies the paper.)

Yes, my children! That's the way! Now listen closely to Papa. We mustn't miss a word. Legibly, please.

(The head of THE MARQUIS *begins to dictate; the hands transcribe.)*

"Let he who questions the truths I tell pay this final story heed. There was once a virtuous man called the Abbé de Coulmier. It was his life's work to cater to the feeble, with a kind heart and a gentle hand. Sometimes, when the sun struck his hair just so, or he tilted his head at a certain angle, you could almost discern the halo that rested there. Then one dark day he encountered a rogue. A rogue with a habit, it seems, for writing stories . . ."

(The head of THE MARQUIS *begins to laugh. The hands twitter and clap with glee. Alone in his cell,* COULMIER *crawls to the window and calls again to the guard.)*

COULMIER: A quill, my good man! A quill! A quill!

(The laughter of THE MARQUIS *echoes up and down the cavernous chambers of the asylum. The inmates join him. The sound of their cackling causes the walls to shake and the floor to roll in waves. Blackout.)*